Poets from the North of Ireland

edited by Frank Ormsby

Blackstaff Press

Published by Blackstaff Press, 255A Upper Newtownards Road,
Belfast BT4 3JF, with the assistance of the Arts Council of Northern
Ireland.
ISBN 0 85640 135 8 (Paper)
ISBN 0 85640 201 X (Cloth)
Cover photograph by Dermott Dunbar.
Printed in Northern Ireland by Belfast Litho Printers Limited.

Preface

This anthology contains selections from twenty Northern poets born since 1900, each of whom has published at least one book-length collection. It does not pretend to be exhaustively representative. A list of absent qualifiers would include John Lyle Donaghy, Robert Greacen, John Irvine, Maurice James Craig, Geoffrey Squires, Francis Harvey and Michael Brophy. A case could be made for the inclusion of Patrick Kavanagh (Co Monaghan), D. J. O'Sullivan (Co Donegal) and George McWhirter (born in Belfast and living in Canada, where his books are published). Of the Northern women poets born since 1900 — Barbara Hunter, Freda Laughton, Meta Mayne Reid and Joan Newmann, for example — few have published in book form. A number of English poets, too, have spent time in the North and written out of their experience there: Philip Larkin, Norman Dugdale, Philip Hobsbaum and Andrew Waterman come to mind.

It is the editor's hope that *Poets from the North of Ireland* will introduce general readers to Northern poetry of the present and the immediate past and that it will gain for the younger poets in par- ticular a wider audience than they could otherwise expect at the beginning of their writing careers. No poet is represented by less than five poems, on the grounds that at least that number is needed to give a reader an adequate sense of a poet's work, and the order of individual selections is, as far as possible, thematic rather than chronological.

Introduction

Written poetry began in the north of Ireland, as elsewhere in the country, with the work of the Bardic poet, or *ollamh*. His patrons were the Gaelic chieftains of such families as the O'Neills, the O'Donnells and the Maguires, for whom he composed eulogies in return for reward and protection and about whom he wrote satires if these were not given. His status was complex. In a country which had adopted Christianity without entirely relinquishing Paganism he was semi-druidic, his social position roughly equivalent to that of a Christian bishop. The power of the *ollamh* declined with the defeat of the native Irish at Kinsale in 1602 and the Flight of the Earls in 1607, but Gaelic poetry continued to be written in the monasteries and elsewhere until the latter part of the eighteenth century. Its final flowering occurred in South Armagh, Cavan, Louth and Meath in the work of such poets as Seamus Dall MacCuarta, Cathal Bui MacGiolla Gunna, Peadar O Doirnin and Art MacCubhthaigh.

Following the Flight of the Earls, the North was colonised by English and Scottish settlers, and the descendants of these groups began to emerge in discernible literary movements at roughly the same time as the Gaelic tradition was dying. The peasant weaver, farmer and schoolmaster poets of south and mid Antrim and north and north-east Down, who flourished at the end of the eighteenth century and in the first half of the nineteenth, had as their literary language a version of Lowlands Scots, and as their poetic exemplars Scottish poets such as Robert Sempill, Sir David Lindsay, Alexander Montgomerie, Allan Ramsay and, of course, Robert Burns. It is appropriate that the peasant poets' names are associated with particular places — James Orr of Ballycarry, Hugh Porter of Moneyslan, James Campbell of Ballynure — for not only did their verse reflect the work, character, customs and everyday existence of the people among whom they lived, but these people gave them

1

patronage in the form of subscriptions to their books. With the movement of the linen industry into the mills and factories, this upsurge of peasant poets lost its impetus and English poetry in the North was left largely in the hands of educated colonials who looked to England for their literary models, though their subjects were sometimes Irish. One group of these, centred around Bishop Thomas Percy at Dromore, Co Down, had flourished concurrently with the peasant poets already mentioned, but Percy died in 1811 and the best colonials outside the Dromore group — Dr William Drennan and James Stuart — in 1820 and 1848 respectively. Northern poetry may be said to survive the century in the work of three Northerners living elsewhere: Sir Samuel Ferguson (1810-86) and Thomas Caulfield Irwin (1823-92) in Dublin, and William Allingham (1824-89) in London.

Ferguson's poetry is significantly transitional. He is the descendant of Scottish planters, but so immersed in the native Irish tradition that he is more nationalistic than colonial. In fact his English imitations of Bardic poems make him an acknowledged precursor of Yeats and the Irish Literary Renaissance, a movement by which the poets associated with the Ulster Literary Theatre in the early years of this century were heavily influenced. George Russell (A.E.) left Ulster to become one of the pillars of the Renaissance, and the work of Alice Milligan, Joseph Campbell and James H. Cousins, for example, reflects the concerns of the Celtic Twilight writers as faithfully as that of the poets in Dublin. By the early 1920s most of the Ulster Literary Theatre poets had left the North or ceased to publish. The period from 1920 to 1930 was a comparatively lean one, most memorable, perhaps, for the dramatic monologues of the linen magnate Richard Rowley, in which he attempts to give dialect voice to Belfast's factory-workers, and for the vigorous 'folk' poetry of the Co Tyrone brothers, W. F. and R. L. Marshall. One could list the decades during which the poets represented in this anthology began to acquire reputations, but to do so would give little sense of the continuity of Northern poetry. Hewitt and Buchanan, for example, wrote poems in the Twenties, did not appear in book-form until 1948 and 1958 respectively, and have both had collections published since 1970; as indeed has every other poet in these pages, if one counts the collected editions of Rodgers (1971) and MacNeice (1979).

When George Buchanan's collection *Bodily Responses* appeared in 1958 he was fifty-four years old and had already published two journals, five novels and a volume of autobiography. *Bodily Responses* and subsequent collections are the work of one who has been finding his way gradually towards a particular subject-matter and style, through the introduction of his central themes in the journals and novels, for example, and the sometimes 'poetic' quality of his prose.

The titles of three of his collections — *Bodily Responses*, *Conversation with Strangers* and *Minute-Book of a City* — are pointers to Buchanan's pervasive concerns. His poems may be seen as salvoes in a campaign against what he calls (in the Preface to *Bodily Responses*) 'aesthetic and emotional impoverishment'. He advocates an intense, receptive awareness of the present moment, a willingness to immerse oneself intelligently and feelingly in the life of one's time and especially in the life of twentieth-century cities. For him the artist is a spiritual revolutionary, an anticipator (a favourite word is 'may') who posits a society in which sensitivity and open-mindedness will replace institutionalized responses, apathy and indifference. He distrusts systems and hierarchies and those who are contemptuous of the masses, rejects aggression and materialism, and prefers an embracing of the 'not-yet-there' to nostalgia for the past. He asks, as in 'War-and-Peace', that life be lived as a dynamic synthesis, a controlled collision with the environment and the instant. Underlying all of these concerns is a vision of human beings as 'world members', and, coupled with his vulnerable belief in this, a determination like that attributed to Lewis Mumford in the poem dedicated to him, to outstare the cynics.

Buchanan is of Scottish Planter descent and grew up in rural Ulster but neither circumstance is directly a subject of much of his poetry. The first considerable laureate of these areas of Ulster experience is John Hewitt. In the Foreword to his *Collected Poems* (1968) he defined himself as 'by birth, an Irishman of Planter stock, by profession an art gallery man, politically a man of the Left', and insisted on the relevance of these facts 'in the conditioning of (his) response to experience'. Six years later, in an *Irish Times* symposium on 'The Clash of Identities' (4th July 1974), he stated his 'hierarchy of values' in the following terms:

> I'm an Ulsterman of Planter stock. I was born in the island of Ireland, so secondly I'm an Irishman. I was born in the British archipelago and English is my native tongue, so I am British. The British archipelago are offshore islands to the continent of Europe, so I'm European.

This lucid statement strongly suggests a man who has thought out his position, who knows where he stands, and to a certain extent this is true to Hewitt; but it is at the point where these certainties end that the tensions of his poetry begin. To be native to a province colonised by one's ancestors, at home and yet 'alien', a city man who loves, but must struggle to relate to, the country, someone aware (as in 'O Country people') of gaps that are finally unbridgeable, is to be perpetually unsure of one's place. Ultimately, then, Hewitt's poetry is a restlessly contemplative, universal quest for self-definition, personally and in relation to society, environment and history.

Louis MacNeice is, like Hewitt, conscious of the factors in his background and upbringing which cut him off from 'the candles of the Irish poor' and is, too, caught in endless cycles of fascination and repulsion in his attitudes to Ireland. Poems about Ireland represent a small fraction of his output and he spent most of his school, university and working life in England, but much of his work is coloured by the experiences of his childhood years in Carrickfergus. Listing influences, he includes 'having been brought up in the north of Ireland, having a father who was a clergyman, the fact that my mother died when I was little'. He mentions also early contacts with mental illness (his mother's) and mental deficiency (he had a mongol brother) and the fact that the house in Carrickfergus was lit by oil-lamps and therefore shadowy, as contributing to the imagery of petrification, fear, anxiety, loneliness and monotony so prevalent in his poetry. They may also, he adds, explain 'an excessive preoccupation in my earlier work with things dazzling, high-coloured quick-moving, hedonistic or up-to-date'.

It is not only in his earlier work that MacNeice is preoccupied with the 'up-to-date'. All his poetic life he was fascinated by the trivia and the most serious issues of his time. This is especially obvious in the poems he wrote in the Thirties, of which decade he was considered one of the leading poets in England with W. H. Auden, Stephen Spender and Cecil Day Lewis. The central concerns of Thirties literature are present in his work: economic decline, unemployment, the rise of Fascism, the Spanish Civil War, the imminence and outbreak of the Second World War. 'Carrickfergus', for example, was written in 1937 and is partly about life lived perpetually in the shadow of twentieth-century wars, and the decline of traditional culture is one serious theme underlying the surface nonsense of 'Bagpipe Music'.

The ominous and disturbing elements in MacNeice's poetry are partly balanced by his joyful recognition of the vigorous plurality of existence, its endless bright assault on the senses, and of the triumphant or forlorn power of love in the face of menace, whether from war or time.

Buchanan and MacNeice were the sons of clergymen and their scepticism and vitality of response to the world are, partly at least, reactions against this background. The same may be said of the poetry of W. R. Rodgers, who was himself a Presbyterian minister for eleven years before leaving the Church to join the BBC. He published only two collections of poems in his lifetime, but his sensuous celebration of the world and the sheer exuberance of his language give his output a meteoric intensity.

In a radio talk entitled 'On Writing a Poem', Rodgers described words as being 'like county councillors: they have always hosts of relations who are looking for employment', and as a poet he was an enthusiastic patron of the linguistic unemployed. Words were his best friends and worst enemies. He could exploit their inherent nepotism to give a startling, highly imaginative, highly infectious picture of, say, a swan or a windy day, but was too often tempted away from his thematic centres into the mere froth of linguistic performance. He is, perhaps, at his most powerful when writing on religious or Biblical themes with a restrained freshness of language, as in 'Lent' and 'The Net' where technical expertise is harnessed and concentrated, or in 'Resurrection. An Easter Sequence' where the diction is comparatively plain, the form loose and the freshness partly a matter of contemporary colloquialism, partly the 'humanizing' effect of this on the figures involved. His best descriptive poetry has what Arnold referred to as 'the power of so dealing with things as to awaken in us a wonderfully full, new, and intimate sense of them, and of our relations with them', and his best religious verse enacts convincingly a drame of joy and austerity, of Puritan values and sensuous affirmation of the world and the flesh, of human and divine.

A distinct progression is evident in Roy McFadden's poetic career. His first two books, published in 1943 and 1945 when he was in his early twenties and informed by a pacifist's awareness of the nightmare of history, are sometimes morbidly elegiac, sometimes marred by a grandiose Yeatsian rhetoric. But even these volumes and especially his third collection, *The Heart's Townland* (1947), in which he expresses some disagreement with the stance and outlook of John Hewitt, show him beginning to develop, stylistically and thematically, along lines laid down by the older poet. Twenty-four years elapsed before the appearance of *The Garryowen* (1971) and one senses that in this book and its successor, *Verifications* (1977), McFadden has belatedly found his way into areas from which he was originally diverted. There is a process of salvage and rediscovery as he presents a past full of people and places in language that no longer threatens to become artificial; and though he is sometimes loosely nostalgic, he shows also an intense imaginative power, particularly in the sequence 'Contemplations of Mary'. His most recent work, which draws its inspiration from his experiences as a solicitor, offers an interesting mixture of professional observation and personal involvement in a subject area unique in Irish poetry.

By the Black Stream, Odour of Blood, Nights in the Bad Place — Padraic Fiacc's titles are as indicative as George Buchanan's of the tone and content of the collections they name. Storm, illness and death, the hardness of industrial Belfast, the violence of Irish history and its shadow over the present are Fiacc's recurring themes and his vision has become increasingly dark. The bulk of his poems have an agonized directness in their treatment of personal and political turmoil and he has been influenced by French and American poetry in his attempt to find suitable technical embodiment for this, with sporadic success. He is at his best in the controlled elegiac cadences of 'Gloss', or when his work is given depth through reference to circumstances and myths beyond the personal and immediate, as in 'Saint Coleman's Song for Flight'. What he essays — the reflection of an unbalanced, tortured society — is, generally, more significant than what he achieves; nevertheless, his voice is entirely his own and he is the earliest poet in this anthology to draw largely for his backgrounds on industrial Belfast, as opposed to the London of Buchanan's and MacNeice's urban poetry.

Introducing his long poem *The Rough Field* in 1972, John Montague wrote that he sometimes saw it 'as taking over where the last bard of the O'Neills left off', and of all the poets of comparable origin represented here, he is the one most conscious of himself as the inheritor of a 'lost tradition', and of the historical events that force him to express his awareness in a 'grafted tongue'. Influenced perhaps by Patrick Kavanagh's poems about Co Monaghan, he was also the first poet from north of the Border this century to write in depth about the rural community in which he grew up. He identifies with the people he describes, but is also sufficiently distanced from them by education to see them not only as individuals but also as representatives of a dying culture. His old women, in particular, are on one level latter-day versions of the female personifications of Ireland common in Gaelic literature. He is both elegist and celebrant. The tone of his rural and historical poems is primarily, but not wholly, one of lament; he is clear-sightedly aware of what was barbaric or limiting in the tradition whose passing he mourns, but he knows even more keenly what vitality and indigenous strength have been lost. He is conscious both of the decay of rural areas and their capacity for adaptation to change. Love, too, is celebrated. In his earliest collections Montague is aware of what is emotionally crippling in·Irish attitudes to love and sex; the honesty and tender sensuality of his own love poetry may be seen not only as personal exploration but as a corrective reaction to such attitudes.

II

The Sixties was a springboard period for poetry in the north of Ireland. One possible reason for this was an increase in the number of educated Catholics, a consequence of the Education Act of 1947. More immediately, the Writers' Group formed by the English poet, Philip Hobsbaum, who was then lecturing at Queen's University, provided a regular opportunity for emerging poets — Seamus Heaney, Michael Longley and James Simmons among them — to read their work and have it criticised. The Group continued to meet for some years after Hobsbaum's departure. In 1965 Michael Emmerson, the Director of the Queen's University Festival, promoted a series of Festival Publications which included the first pamphlet collections of Heaney, Longley, Simmons, Derek Mahon and Seamus Deane. Harry Chambers' magazine *Phoenix* (1965-75), the first few issues of which appeared from Belfast, reinforced these; and in 1968 James Simmons founded *The Honest Ulsterman* magazine, which became an outlet for the poets already mentioned and for generations of their successors. The Arts Council of Northern Ireland responded by granting subsidies to various publications and by promoting reading tours; the first was *Room to Rhyme* (1968), with Heaney, Longley and the folk-singer David Hammond, and it has been followed in the Seventies by *The Planter and the Gael* (1970-71), with Hewitt and Montague, *Out of the Blue* (1974), with Simmons and Muldoon and *In their Element* (1977), with Heaney and Mahon.

James Simmons' stance is that of the reformer or secular evangelist who is firmly on the side of life and freedom, but who possesses an ironic self-awareness. The drama of his poetry often lies in the pitting of theory against personal experience and human fallibility, especially in the areas of love, sex, marriage, the family, growing old. Not only is he engaged in exploring the quicksands of passion, joy, possessiveness, jealousy, betrayal, emotional dishonesty, unhappiness, but also in a campaign against the elitist image and minority attraction of poetry. Simmons is a writer and singer of songs as well as a poet and his poetry aspires to the accessibility and popular appeal of song. He does not always avoid the dangers of over-simplicity, indulgent confessionalism and flatness of style which are inherent in his approach, but his best poems have a startling direct-ness that clarifies the complexity of life without reducing it, a note of sympathy and celebration, a convincing sense of how people can, to adapt his own words, muddle through to ecstasy or revelation. The quotidian and the banal are the material of Simmons' poetry, but because he sees life and literature as inseparably linked he can make fertile use of characters from *King Lear* and *The Tempest*, for example, as a means of self-analysis, or use art as an illuminating perspective on reality, and vice versa.

A consolidating factor in the poetic activity of the Sixties already described was the immediate success of Seamus Heaney's first collection, *Death of a Naturalist* (1966). The opening poem is called 'Digging' and it establishes Heaney as the new explorer of territories charted by Montague. His education has isolated him from his rural background, but he is constantly aware of his poetry as a craft akin to the traditional crafts of turf-cutter, ploughman, thatcher, water-diviner, salmon-fisher, mummer and blacksmith. The poem esta-blishes also his characteristic use of rich, muscular language to convey the sights, sounds and feel of the countryside, the awareness prevalent in his poetry of digging as a metaphor for personal and historical exploration and his interest in bogland, which he comes to see in later poems as a bottomless preserver of the past. His reading of the Danish archaeologist P. V. Glob's book *The Bog People*, about the sacrificial victims of fertility rites in Scandinavia, has led Heaney, in his collections *Wintering Out* (1972) and *North* (1975), to attempt an illumination of Irish, and especially Ulster history, in terms of these tribal mores, though in *North* he also approaches the Ulster situation from the standpoint of personal experience. There is an increasing range of cultural reference in Heaney's poetry — to literature, history, art, mythology — and though he usually incorporates it effortlessly he is, as a poet, akin to the figure from classical myth who laid significantly early claim to his imagination — Antaeus, who wrestled with Hercules and whose strength was renewed at every contact with the earth.

Michael Longley's *No Continuing City* (1969) is more daunting in its allusive range. Circe, Nausicaa, Persephone and Narcissus rub shoulders with Walter Mitty, Emily Dickinson, John Clare, Dr. Johnson, Rip Van Winkle, Fats Waller, Bud Freeman, Bessy Smith and Bix Beiderbecke, to mention only those who appear by name, but the cast are brought consistently into immediate relationship with the reader, technically through the use of apostrophe and dramatic monologue, most profoundly in the way they are discovered to represent the universally human in their attitudes, feelings and situations. This book and Longley's two subsequent collections, which are less specifically allusive, illustrate his ability to approach experience obliquely through frameworks of myth, culture, mystique, or in a more directly personal manner, as in 'In Memoriam' and 'Wounds' and some of his love poems. He is not as obsessively concerned with Irish history as are, say, Montague and Heaney, but he shows an awareness, especially in *An Exploded View* (1973), of cultural divisions in Ireland, of himself as an ineffectual observer on the fringe of events, but also of the importance of poetry as one of the repositories of positive and civilized values in a time of chaos. Longley's skill as a technician finds expression in the longer poem with complicated stanza forms, the short poem which depends for effect on a few resonant images, and the verse letter.

Although Seamus Deane's first book, *Gradual Wars*, did not appear until 1972, he was a contemporary of Seamus Heaney at Queen's University and Festival Publications had issued a pamphlet

9

by him in 1966. *Gradual Wars* contains evocations of history-haunted, trouble-torn Derry, its recurrent persona a menaced figure among faces that loom out of nightmares, murderous shadows on the wall and the sound of sirens. Like so many other poets anthologised here, Deane is caught between the unhappiness in his native place that threatens to stifle him and the profound attraction and even necessity of roots. In this book, and in *Rumours* (1977), he deals also with love and the family, sometimes with an impassioned, sometimes with a clinically image-making, intelligence.

Derek Mahon's poetry is smitten with the restlessness of cities, the figures who inhabit it constantly in transit, between life and death, control and chaos, one place and another. His confident wit and assured cadences function ironically as surface stabilities over unsettled depths but also as affirmations of art as a possible source of order, however inadequate, to set against all that is dauntingly 'unstructurable'. Mahon is particularly conscious of the abyss that underlies the materialistic solidities of middle-class existence. He understands and identifies with the alienated — Dowson, de Quincey, Van Gogh, Edvard Munch, characters from Beckett — recognising how preferable to mindless complacency their lives can be, but also how difficult and tortured. Ireland usually figures in his poetry as a point of arrival or departure, a place from which he wishes to escape but which refuses to be exorcised, another ground on which he is drawn into the quest for equilibrium which informs his work. His vision of 'civilization' in decline is balanced by an awareness of painful persistence and survival, the darkness in his poetry always struggling towards or emerging into its complement of light. He is the intelligent observer who realises the dangers of knowing too much 'To be anything any more', the elegist who ultimately refuses to mourn.

III

Poets from the north of Ireland have always sought publication for their poems and books outside Belfast and a comprehensive list of their outlets would include the leading British and Irish journals and publishing houses of their periods. The first locally-published magazine of any significance this century was *Uladh* (1904-05), the organ of the Ulster Literary Theatre. The next two were *Lagan* (1943-46), edited by John Boyd, and *Rann* (1948-53), edited by Roy McFadden and Barbara Hunter, both of which published, among others, MacNeice, Rodgers and Hewitt. *Threshold* was founded in 1957 and still appears sporadically. There have been numerous other, usually short-lived, magazines, but the only regular platform in recent times has been *The Honest Ulsterman*, of which over sixty numbers have appeared since 1968. In that period it has included not only the work of established Northern poets but the first or early poems of Ciaran Carson, Michael Foley, Tom Matthews, Paul Muldoon, Frank Ormsby, Tom Paulin and William Peskett, and the first pamphlet collections of all these poets have appeared in the magazine's companion series of Ulsterman Publications. The most prominent local publisher of book-length collections is the Blackstaff Press, founded in 1971; its list includes volumes by John Hewitt, Roy McFadden, Padraic Fiacc, James Simmons, Michael Foley, Ciaran Carson and Gerald Dawe.

If Tom Matthews' idiosyncratic poetry may be said to have a model it is surely the work of the English poet, Stevie Smith. Beneath its deceptive spareness and simplicity it is elusively alive to small sufferings, complexes, embarrassments, marginal alienations. It provides a refuge for such as Gustav the Great Explorer, who is not himself unless he has his snowboots on, Giorgio the Juggler from Bolton whose audience applauds 'in desperation', the poet with bad teeth to whom an appearance-conscious public is not prepared to listen. Matthews presents the lonely, the odd and the failures in a way that sometimes tickles our sense of the absurd but stirs our sympathy as well.

Michael Foley too has a sense of the absurd. His viewpoint is often that of the wide-eyed, sharply watchful provincial-at-large, testing his preconceptions and expectations against experience. The poems in *True Life Love Stories* (1976) swing brashly between extravagant fantasy and an ironic self-debunking; they draw on such sources as film, comic-strip, jazz, bawdy idiom, literary quotation (accurate and distorted), for their headlong energy: Among the targets of Foley's iconoclastic humour are teachers and orthodox education, the preciousness or stodginess of some poetry, the timidity of family and middle-class attitudes, materialism, social-climbing. In him the quiet voice associated with Northern poetry turns sardonic and cynical or rises to a bellow. Life and literature are important, but to be taken with a bucket of salt, and he is almost apologetic for his moments of tenderness.

Foley helped edit *The Honest Ulsterman* for a time with its present

11

editor, Frank Ormsby. The latter's earliest work, which is set among the small farms and village housing-estates of Co. Fermanagh, deals with the practicality and reticence of country people and their attachment to place, probing beneath the placid surfaces of their lives. In these poems, and also in those with urban settings, his awareness of division and upheaval is balanced by a desire to trust in traditional stabilities and human resilience, though he recognises that such trust is not always possible. He sees private lives as sometimes blighted by public events, or as flourishing toughly or serenely in spite of them.

Foley, Ormsby and Muldoon are three more examples of educated Northern Irish Catholics growing away from their background but finding their poetry permeated by its attitudes, traditions, and minority status. The same may be said of Ciaran Carson, whose upbringing was bilingual. The monastic side of the Gaelic tradition is the inspiration behind the St Ciaran poems in *The New Estate* (1976), but he can also write about Belfast with a sense of its industrial past and present, its housing estates and its violence. Craftsmen figure prominently in his poems: the scribe, weaver, bell-caster, fiddler, chimney-sweep, house-painter, bomb-disposal expert. Stillness, coldness, silence, sickness, death, the loneliness and the consoling simplicities of isolation, household ritual, tensions and distances within the family are among the subjects he treats with his own delicate mixture of craft and feeling.

Tom Paulin sees cities and states as potentially efficient but capable of carrying efficiency to a point where they are indifferent to individual existence. His people survive or pioneer in a world of industrial bleakness with undercurrents and upsurges of violence, or among the ruthless, divisive simplicities of politics, religion, class. They are cautious or austere in their relationships, their security often as much a matter of limitation as safety. There is a harsh vein in many of Paulin's poems, compounded of the details that convey a sense of the steel/metal/concrete realities of city life and the poet's indignation at injustice and exploitation.

Paul Muldoon is the most ambitious and technically assured of the younger Northern poets. His best poems turn on subtleties and shocks in the area between innocence and experience, love as rapacious or going sour or shading into tension, place as a repository of tradition, background as a shaping influence on the self, guilt and allegiance and responsibility. They are idiomatic and ambiguous and sometimes obscure, at pains to convey the complexity of the ordinary in rhythms and language which bring it freshly to our perceptions. Muldoon is an inhabitant of The Moy, The World, The Universe.

The North of Gerald Dawe's *Sheltering Places* (1978) is urban and comprehensively 'Black', in its industrialisation and its violent inheritance from history. Blood, darkness and storm are as pervasive as in the poetry of Padraic Fiacc, and though emigration is considered as a possible means of escape it is also seen as a kind of evasion. There is little optimism or consolation in the poems. At the end of 'Physical Environment', for example, Northerners are depicted as growing to live with their native place, but in the light of the whole poem one is left with an impression of negative resignation on their part as much as of a positive coping. The people in Dawe's poetry tend to be haunted and rootless, on the move, bereft of certainties. Their 'sheltering places' give no guarantee of shelter.

William Peskett had, like Michael Foley, a scientific education, and it bears on his poems to an extent that Foley's does not. Peskett's work deals with detachment and impersonality, a clinical future in which the mysteries of the natural world (symbolised a number of times by the night-owl) may be diminished, with inheritance, with the contrast between natural and artificial worlds. He is aware and weary of the limitations of scientific knowledge and has a related affection and reverence for plants and animals. His humans are often insignificant figures against impersonal backdrops of history, time, the cosmos, though the couple in 'Window Dressing' are exceptions.

IV

The poets represented here have been praised for constant resourcefulness in the use of traditional forms, and accused of being technically unadventurous, unwilling to experiment, prisoners of the neat lyric. They have been commended for their restraint in not allowing the brutal realities of their place and time to impair their sense of aesthetic responsibility, and denounced for failure to 'confront' the realities directly. It has been said that their imaginative lives have, to an extent, been 'limited by the horizons defined by the colonial predicament' of the North, and, on another level, that too many of them are 'insulated in some university shelter-belt or ... ensconced in some cultural oasis such as the Arts Council or the BBC' and therefore cut off from the majority of ordinary lives. Their qualities of common sense and down-to-earthness have been approved as sources of strength, and deplored as factors that hold their imagination back from flight. This anthology gives the reader an opportunity to decide for himself.

GEORGE BUCHANAN b. 1904

Lyle Donaghy, poet, 1902-1949

The product of peoples on two sides of a narrow sea,
he was raised with his head full of half-naked Greeks.
His rainy countryside didn't, scholastically, exist.
Under a tree he heard drums with their heavy beat
recommend a dislike which he didn't share.

He watched from a window the rain splashing
and after the rain the treedrip on the river.
His poem, a slow adding of words,
grew with a lack of urgency as trees grow.
The mind exudes stuff, not in sentences
baked to a style, but softly. Sir,
I don't address you in precious stones.

He heard clergy shouting from pulpits against
the sins of the body. Schooled in the prime
material of flowering girls and trees
he loved—poet-wise—poet-foolish—
with ex-puritan extravagance.

Turning a boulder in the grass, laughing
at the insects, he was filled with Whitman energy
as a train puffed by on the narrow-gauge.

Where do we go to find the evenings
which late sunshine on saplings used to make?
He piled stones savagely for a house for himself
in a valley, cautious about the trees,
not sinking to their calm, wanting to utter
a cry clear of the lake, an abstract
artifice beyond the natural liberties;
undid the academic ropes, waited for the surge.

Conversation With Strangers

Strangers are people we haven't seen before,
the herbage of urban meadows. They're
unexplored countries. A greeting could expose
a fresh geography.

We open the door, go into the blue. The glance of others
is a sunlight. If we don't perceive them
we're without insight or sick. For everyone's invited
to be known: the new knowledge. It may be ignorance
that prevents us from loving our neighbours.

Too facile speaking betrays misery. We're sorry for gabblers
in a public place. We find it hard ourselves
to open our lips, being ponderous from past suffering.

We were reared in privacy, off the street, out of earshot.
'Oh no strangers, please! Only people we know!'

```
PRIVATE
KEEP OUT
```

This notice was pinned to the door. Let nobody look over the garden
  gate.
They also said: 'Don't refer to this or that in front of the child.'
                            We became shy,
nervous of the great world. 'Don't speak to strangers,' they said.
It seemed starving strangers were waiting to catch at sensual
  straws, even
the unsatisfactory bodies of children.

Secrecy was praised. 'Don't visibly enjoy yourself. Find a hotel
apart from the crowd. Swim in a deserted bay. Be careful
what you say on the important subjects: better still, avoid them.
Give copious information on holidays, weather and sport; but hide
  your love
and your hate; seem to have a temperature of zero.'

Over against this was JC's message from Palestine
about loving people to whom we haven't been formally introduced.

Easiness with one another would show that the message is heard.
Citizens wouldn't be afraid of making asses of themselves.

Can we de-house and evict ourselves from our solid homes;
a break-out is due. Radio, newspaper
pierce the shell of the house. Ah the relief
as the walls are pierced. Let's be unafraid
if the cameras come, if we're declared open to the public.

Like a girl on the stage who uncovers and states her essence,
we also expose ourselves: our naked fact is our unity.
All inhabitants are joined, even those who don't know it.
Those others are us; they must be hard to despise or kill.
We rear a joint city with a shared construction, hurrying builders,
    the tink of hammers.
But our ambition can come about only if we imagine our union.

Sneering at the sheer number of others is a drug for self-cultivators
who are also (they won't believe it) particles of the mass.
All of us are; and are filled with that million-made blaze.
Up it comes and burns through us.
As passengers of a train, shoppers, part of an audience,
we notice and are pleased to be with the rest.
Gone the bowing and scraping, the abject public, unworthy to
    come in.

The broken big-wigs, military heroes, so-called geniuses
are on show like deserted castles: a penny a peep!
The struggle to reclassify ourselves as top men or stars
isn't on. Our study isn't to reach a tower
but go deep like Orpheus into the general world,
to be unguarded with others.

In the park, please, no vilification of many in one place.
If we're world members we can't stiffen as others walk past us,
can't make faces of triumph or fear. Women sit in chairs; a
    grey-haired lady
shows her legs as one might mention a former wealth;

dandyish young lie under trees. There are bubbles
of affection in the long afternoon. The cold society
we used to know is almost dying. Strangers may cease to be
    strangers.
We may go to the park as to a room of (near) friends.

War-and-Peace

War is the angry man waving his desperate
    weapon,
the mushroom cloud in the Pacific Ocean.

Peace is quietude for retired persons sitting on
    fixed principles, sealed off from the climate of
    the contingent in a place where nothing is
    urgent:
life arranged for academic study, isolated, sub-
    divided, known, a subject on which X and Y
    may be taken as the recognised authorities.
It is that evening hymn full of tiredness and repose
    and low, stop-worrying voices, the reverend
    boredom.
It is an eternal luxury cruise in the sun with bingo
    at night after a heavy dinner.
Ideal circumstance, the advertised article, expensive
    ease:
a dream of summoning perfect waiters to the
    table with a small upward movement of
    the eyes.

There is neither war nor peace, there is war-*and*-
    peace, not either/or but the two:

rather, if you please, fusion, the play of one into
   the other, the blend.
War-and-peace isn't either anger or stillness, but
   persons moving in the great event of their
   city every day.
Not peace of mind but the troubled mind:
the warman on the peace path, the peaceman on
   the war path.
It is the impure joy, the dream and the awakening,
   the two sides of the medal:
the anxious holiday, the sunny tour of an Italian
   lake with a sick girl,
the extravagance of an unhappy time in a delectable
   but costly place,
friction in the country drawingroom with an out-
   look of trees,
the senescence and poverty of a great public figure,
the evil politics of a new and exquisitely laid-out
   town.
It is co-operation with disliked persons, not segregation
   or party alignment,
but swallowing resentment, working with detested
   characters, undertaking a keen enterprise with
   untrustworthy associates;
talking of god's love with a bad-tempered clergy-
   man;
drinking a fine claret holding the glass with fingers from
   which torturers have drawn the nails;
coming home after dark to a divided family, living
   in harmony with a bitch.

I Suddenly...

I suddenly have come to love
you who have been no more than friend
so long and constantly...
                              I am
a traveller startled that the end
of stormy questing in a ship
for lands of mystery should be
to sight the blue smoke of his home
and anchor at his native quay.

Song for Straphangers

I bought a red-brick villa
   and dug the garden round
because a young girl smiled in June:
   in August we were bound
      by a marriage vow,
      and then till now
I count up every pound.

I count up every penny,
   I work and never cease,
because a young girl smiled in June
   and there is no release.
      Sometimes I swear
      it's most unfair.
Sometimes I feel at peace.

21

Revolutionary Revolution

Insidious in ways no gunfire touches, revolution
must have revolution in it too,
not be the same old murder.

The cry for a tender
style has never been so truly from the heart,
so treated as nothing much.

Knowledge-workers

'I know something, therefore I am.'
For knowledge one went to the sea-bed,
one, dressed in fur, to an icefloe,
one turned to what the leaves were up to,
one took photographs of the beating heart.
Scholar-gentry sought beauties
of colour under the plaster of twelfth
century walls. Discover, explain:
clouds of knowing were over the island.

Praise was once given to the deep men.
Their expression, principally through the eyes,
told they were absent on the profundity track,
so loaded with erudition they could hardly think.
Consider, friends, we carry a shallow message.
Dress-style is a matter of serious brainwork
and the shortness of a skirt is what is called an idea.

The Cabinet

Absence of ideas in the Cabinet. Dust fell
from the ceiling in a slow shower. They rang and sent
for another basket of statistics. Could no one find
the document which would increase the amount of hope?
The poets' message read: 'If we're to avoid disaster
it may be enough to make existence attractive.'
The Prime Minister walked crossly to the window.
'Pleasure! Are they cuckoo?' He smacked one
clenched hand into the other. 'We must be tough!'

So the government keep to the normal style,
to the icy water. Scolding and fretting, they dream
of spectacular counterthrusts.

A Speaker in the Square

We hear her in the square. At two o'clock
fawn moths in thousands enter shops and cars.
There's a rush to shut the windows. Then
she steps to the platform without the brazen bearing
of usual parliament men. She can't do
miracles and sway the crowd; make listeners
advocates. She is heard
less for what she says than for her tossing
hair. Her love is to ideas,
the devastating love. Richness of feeling
is the prosperity she advocates.
'We won't permit a frozen future
or a manipulated one. Rebel.
Not by knifing constables, filling
the square with shots. No military coup.
Only a rise in temperature.

Freedom isn't freedom if people are cold.
Truth isn't truth if told by citizens
who don't care. We need an illumination
from glances. Human sunlight...'

Newspapers say it's true: WAR IS OFF.
For how long? History hasn't yet related.
Can the Prime Minister stay in office if
no war is threatened? He faces novel problems
when the electors aren't too deeply worried.
Without a mandate to be frivolous
he feels he must resign.

Author of elegant iambics, she
comes in a wintry moment, melts the ice
in a masculine country famous for reserve,
is carried to power by a flock of writers.
The Poetic State is founded.

A Churchman Speaks

'Cultivate monotony by repeated prayers.
Surrendering to that ennui, get strength.
The drone of sleepy hymns, the unoriginal
sermons serve a purpose. The Eternal
has seen enough of men to know by now
the nature of the case, may also suffer
a rather experienced boredom. We've little time
for saints or fanatics. Perhaps God too prefers
Christians who've cooled their zeal.'

Lewis Mumford

He has an eye for cities. Among his rows
of vegetables he dreams of cloistered squares
where people ruminate or meet without
being made nervous of a stream of cars.
This shocks the men who care for motor-speed
more than spontaneous interchange. They think
only a mind inadequately trained
would advocate a nice humanity.
But someone must, and he outstares the cynics.
The cause is worth it. His eager mind, employing
evidence from history, enters on
a massive disquisition to preserve
affectionate glances, tenderness in sips.

Advancing Years

The well-worn but alarming week goes through him.
He wakes and walks out over areas
mined for incautious steps. The house he lives in
is a bubble. He is more helpless than when born:
there's no attentive parent; friends and children
absent. In growing a grey or a white beard
has he wasted time? He is reproached
'you could have…' as the showers fall on a dry
street and the windows. Full of regret, he turns
towards one more summer. Will he plunge
in sea water by a hot island? The hotels offer
shoreline gazing from a well-placed chair,
a table for one in the long dining room.

JOHN HEWITT b. 1907

I Write For...

I write for my own kind,
I do not pitch my voice
that every phrase be heard
by those who have no choice:
their quality of mind
must be withdrawn and still,
as moth that answers moth
across a roaring hill.

Once Alien Here

Once alien here my fathers built their house,
claimed, drained, and gave the land the shapes of use,
and for their urgent labour grudged no more
than shuffled pennies from the hoarded store
of well rubbed words that had left their overtones
in the ripe England of the mounded downs.

The sullen Irish limping to the hills
bore with them the enchantments and the spells
that in the clans' free days hung gay and rich
on every twig of every thorny hedge,
and gave the rain-pocked stone a meaning past
the blurred engraving of the fibrous frost.

So I, because of all the buried men
in Ulster clay, because of rock and glen
and mist and cloud and quality of air
as native in my thought as any here,
who now would seek a native mode to tell
our stubborn wisdom individual,
yet lacking skill in either scale of song,

27

the graver English, lyric Irish tongue,
must let this rich earth so enhance the blood
with steady pulse where now is plunging mood
till thought and image may, identified,
find easy voice to utter each aright.

An Irishman in Coventry

A full year since, I took this eager city,
the tolerance that laced its blatant roar,
its famous steeples and its web of girders,
as image of the state hope argued for,
and scarcely flung a bitter thought behind me
on all that flaws the glory and the grace
which ribbons through the sick, guilt-clotted legend
of my creed-haunted, Godforsaken race.
My rhetoric swung round from steel's high promise
to the precision of the well-gauged tool,
tracing the logic in the vast glass headlands,
the clockwork horse, the comprehensive school.

Then, sudden, by occasion's chance concerted,
in enclave of my nation, but apart,
the jigging dances and the lilting fiddle
stirred the old rage and pity in my heart.
The faces and the voices blurring round me,
the strong hands long familiar with the spade,
the whiskey-tinctured breath, the pious buttons,
called up a people endlessly betrayed
by our own weakness, by the wrongs we suffered
in that long twilight over bog and glen,
by force, by famine and by glittering fables

which gave us martyrs when we needed men,
by faith which had no charity to offer,
by poisoned memory, and by ready wit,
with poverty corroded into malice,
to hit and run and howl when it is hit.

This is our fate: eight hundred years' disaster,
crazily tangled as the Book of Kells;
the dream's distortion and the land's division,
the midnight raiders and the prison cells.
Yet like Lir's children banished to the waters
our hearts still listen for the landward bells.

The Scar

for Padriac Fiacc

There's not a chance now that I might recover
one syllable of what that sick man said,
tapping upon my great-grandmother's shutter,
and begging, I was told, a piece of bread;
for on his tainted breath there hung infection
rank from the cabins of the stricken west,
the spores from black potato-stalks, the spittle
mottled with poison in his rattling chest;
but she who, by her nature, quickly answered,
accepted in return the famine-fever;
and that chance meeting, that brief confrontation,
conscribed me of the Irishry forever.

Though much I cherish lies outside their vision,
and much they prize I have no claim to share,
yet in that woman's death I found my nation;
the old wound aches and shews its fellow-scar.

A Father's Death

It was no vast dynastic fate
when gasp by gasp my father died,
no mourners at the palace gate,
or tall bells tolling slow and wide.

We sat beside the bed; the screen
shut out the hushed, the tiptoe ward,
and now and then we both would lean
to catch what seemed a whispered word.

My mother watched her days drag by,
two score and five the married years,
yet never weakened to a cry
who was so ready with her tears.

Then, when dawn washed the polished floor
and steps and voices woke and stirred
with wheels along the corridor,
my father went without a word.

The sick, the dying, bed by bed,
lay clenched around their own affairs;
that one behind a screen was dead
was someone's grief, but none of theirs.

It was no vast dynastic death,
no nation silent round that throne,
when, letting go his final breath,
a lonely man went out alone.

O Country People

O country people, you of the hill farms,
huddled so in darkness I cannot tell
whether the light across the glen is a star,
or the bright lamp spilling over the sill,
I would be neighbourly, would come to terms
with your existence, but you are so far;
there is a wide bog between us, a high wall.
I've tried to learn the smaller parts of speech
in your slow language, but my thoughts need more
flexible shapes to move in, if I am to reach
into the hearth's red heart across the half-door.

You are coarse to my senses, to my washed skin;
I shall maybe learn to wear dung on my heel,
but the slow assurance, the unconscious discipline
informing your vocabulary of skill,
is beyond my mastery, who have followed a trade
three generations now, at counter and desk;
hand me a rake, and I at once, betrayed,
will shed more sweat than is needed for the task.

If I could gear my mind to the year's round,
take season into season without a break,
instead of feeling my heart bound and rebound
because of the full moon or the first snowflake,
I should have gained something. Your secret is pace.
Already in your company I can keep step,
but alone, involved in a headlong race,
I never know the moment when to stop.

I know the level you accept me on,
like a strange bird observed about the house,
or sometimes seen out flying on the moss
that may tomorrow, or next week, be gone,
liable to return without warning
on a May afternoon and away in the morning.

But we are no part of your world, your way,
as a field or a tree is, or a spring well.
We are not held to you by the mesh of kin;
we must always take a step back to begin,
and there are many things you never tell
because we would not know the things you say.

I recognize the limits I can stretch;
even a lifetime among you should leave me strange,
for I could not change enough, and you will not change;
there'd still be levels neither'd ever reach.
And so I cannot ever hope to become,
for all my goodwill toward you, yours to me,
even a phrase or a story which will come
pat to the tongue, part of the tapestry
of apt response, at the appropriate time,
like a wise saw, a joke, an ancient rime
used when the last stack's topped at the day's end,
or when the last lint's carted round the bend.

From the Tibetan

In my native province when I was young
the lamas were presumed to be dishonest,
not because they were more wicked than the rest
but their calling gave them more scope.

They were not expected to be philosophers
or poets, for they were not educated persons;
theories were as inconceivable as books
in their satchels. All they were asked
was to provide certain familiar noises

on fixed occasions of the calendar,
spinning the wheels with ritual fervour
and chanting of *The Emperor's Tunic*
and *The Great Wall of China.*

For the rest of their time it was anticipated
that they should work hard rewarding their families,
promoting their nephews, replenishing their stores,
and accepting presents from contractors.
Traditionally, all this was to be done with a show
of cordiality, with handclasps, salutes,
conspicuous finger-signals and audible passwords:
the effect which it was desired to produce
being that of reluctant necessity
for complicated manoeuvre.

Now I am older and live in the suburbs of the capital,
I find that the lamas here are very much the same,
save that the rewarding, promoting, replenishing, is
done on their behalf by a permanent secretariat,
leaving them more time to devote to the illusion
of exercising power: this forces them to acquire
a more sophisticated vocabulary; indeed,
one or two of them have written books:
in my native province this
would have been looked upon with disfavour,
for we are a simple people.

The King's Horses

After fifty years, nearly, I remember,
living then in a quiet leafy suburb,
waking in the darkness, made aware
of a continuous irregular noise,
and groping to the side-window to discover
the shadow-shapes which made that muffled patter
passing across the end of our avenue,
the black trees and the streetlights shuttering
a straggle of flowing shadows, endless, of horses.

Gypsies they could have been, or tinkers maybe,
mustering to some hosting of their clans,
or horse-dealers heading their charges to the docks
timed to miss the day's traffic and alarms;
a migration the newspapers had not foretold;
some battle's ragged finish, dream repeated;
the last of an age retreating, withdrawing,
leaving us beggared, bereft
of the proud nodding muzzles, the nervous bodies;
gone from us the dark men with their ancient skills
of saddle and stirrup, of bridle and breeding.

It was an end, I was sure, but an end of what
I never could tell. It was never reported;
but the echoing hooves persisted. Years after,
in a London hotel in the grey dawn
a serious man concerned with certain duties,
I heard again the metal clatter of hooves staccato
and hurriedly rose to catch a glimpse of my horses,
but the pace and beat were utterly different:
I saw by the men astride these were the King's horses
going about the King's business, never mine.

The Search
for Shirley and Darryl

We left the western island to live among strangers
in a city older by centuries
than the market town which we had come from
where the slow river spills out between green hills
and gulls perch on the bannered poles.

It is a hard responsibility to be a stranger;
to hear your speech sounding at odds with your neighbours;
holding your tongue from quick comparisons;
remembering that you are a guest in the house.

Often you will regret the voyage,
wakening in the dark night to recall that other place
or glimpsing the moon rising and recollecting
that it is also rising over named hills,
shining on known waters.

But sometimes the thought
that you have not come away from, but returned,
to this older place whose landmarks are yours also,
occurs when you look down a long street remarking
the architectural styles or move through a landscape
with wheat ripening in large fields.

Yet you may not rest here, having come back,
for this is not your abiding place, either.

The authorities declare that in former days
the western island was uninhabited,
just as where you reside now was once tundra,
and what you seek maybe no more than
a broken circle of stones on a rough hillside, somewhere.

Because I Paced My Thought

Because I paced my thought by the natural world,
the earth organic, renewed with the palpable seasons,
rather than the city falling ruinous, slowly
by weather and use, swiftly by bomb and argument,

I found myself alone who had hoped for attention.
If one listened a moment he murmured his dissent:
this is an idle game for a cowardly mind.
The day is urgent. The sun is not on the agenda.

And some who hated the city and man's unreasoning acts
remarked: He is no ally. He does not say that
Power and Hate are the engines of human treason.
There is no answering love in the yellowing leaf.

I should have made it plain that I stake my future
on birds flying in and out of the schoolroom-window,
on the council of sunburnt comrades in the sun,
and the picture carried with singing into the temple.

The Ram's Horn

I have turned to the landscape because men disappoint me:
the trunk of a tree is proud; when the woodmen fell it,
it still has a contained ionic solemnity:
it is a rounded event without the need to tell it.

I have never been compelled to turn away from the dawn
because it carries treason behind its wakened face:
even the horned ram, glowering over the bog-hole,
though symbol of evil, will step through the blown grass
    with grace.

Animal, plant, or insect, stone or water,
are, every minute, themselves; they behave by law.
I am not required to discover motives for them,
or strip my heart to forgive the rat in the straw.

I live my best in the landscape, being at ease there;
the only trouble I find I have brought in my hand.
See, I let it fall with a rustle of stems in the nettles,
and never for a moment suppose that they understand.

Substance and Shadow

There is a bareness in the images
I temper time with in my mind's defence;
they hold their own, their stubborn secrecies;
no use to rage against their reticence:-
a gannet's plunge, a heron by a pond,
a last rook homing as the sun goes down,
a spider squatting on a bracken-frond,
and thistles in a cornsheaf's tufted crown,
a boulder on a hillside, lichen-stained,
the sparks of sun on dripping icicles,
their durable significance contained
in texture, colour, shape, and nothing else.
All these are sharp, spare, simple, native to
this small republic I have charted out
as the sure acre where my sense is true,
while round its boundaries sprawl the screes of doubt.

My lamp lights up the kettle on the stove
and throws its shadow on the white-washed wall,
like some Assyrian profile with, above,

a snake- or bird-prowed helmet crested tall;
but this remains a shadow; when I shift
the lamp or move the kettle it is gone,
the substance and the shadow break adrift
that needed bronze to lock them, bronze or stone.

The Moon

Now from our village we regard the moon
prime satellite, that some have visited,
a place like Venice but more surely dead,
with less to offer at its broadest noon
than thirty seconds here in any June;
its sole surprise the black sky overhead;
this, after all the peering poets said,
will mean no more than buoy or bollard soon.

Now stripped of mischief if it's glimpsed through glass,
a neutral disc henceforth, although its light
lays waning magic on tree-shadowed grass,
that fabulous tub of myth and metaphor
still rules the seas with undiminished might
and daily hurls the tide against the shore.

Et tu in Arcadia Vixisti

for Roberta

You woke me, rising—this in Paris once—
I watched you stepping—thirty years ago—
to the long window—Many such we've since
unshuttered back from narrow streets below,
but on no more than stir of wheel or foot—
as, finger-signalled, following, I stood
beside you, heeding, drifting up, a flute-
like music, blown through the clean hollow wood,
while, leaning, a dark lad against the wall
played to the splay of goats about his knees,
strayed, so it seemed, from classic pastoral,
an instant's magic—never ours in Greece,
when, later, older, or in Sicily,
we stood, at dawn, beside the tideless sea.

from Sonnets for Roberta (1954)

I

How have I served you? I have let you waste
the substance of your summer on my mood;
the image of the woman is defaced,
and some mere chattel-thing of cloth and wood
performs the household rites, while I, content,
mesh the fine words to net the turning thought,
or eke the hours out, gravely diligent,
to draw to sight that which, when it is brought,
is seldom worth the labour, while you wait,
the little loving gestures held at bay,
each mocking moment inappropriate
for pompous duty never stoops to play;
yet sometimes, at a pause, I recognise
the lonely pity in your lifted eyes.

II

If I had given you that love and care
I long have lavished with harsh loyalty
on some blurred concept spun of earth and air
and real only in some bird or tree,
then you had lived in every pulse and tone
and found the meaning in the wine and bread
who have been forced to walk these ways alone,
my dry thoughts droning always on ahead.
Then you had lived as other women live,
warmed by a touch, responsive to a glance,
glad to endure, so that endurance give
the right to share each changing circumstance,
and yet, for all my treason, you were true
to me, as I to something less than you.

A Birthday Rhyme for Roberta
October 1904—October 1975

For ease of heart and mind
I estimate each stride,
and, lurching forward, find
the landmarks still abide
though senses be decayed,
blurred sight and muffled sound.
Yet yesterday I strayed
on acorn-gravelled ground
to find October true
by each diminished sense,
perpetually new
as grace or innocence.

But now not with me there
picking the coloured leaves,
was she I thought must share
the thistles and the sheaves
when this late harvesting
my husbandry may prove,
as she had shared the spring
and summer of my love.

A Local Poet

He followed their lilting stanzas
through a thousand columns or more,
and scratched for the splintered couplets
in the cracks on the cottage floor,
for his Rhyming Weavers fell silent
when they flocked through the factory door.

He'd imagined a highway of heroes
and stepped aside on the grass
to let Cuchullain's chariot through,
and the Starry Ploughmen pass;
but he met the Travelling Gunman
instead of the Gallowglass.

And so, with luck, for a decade
down the widowed years ahead,
the pension which crippled his courage
will keep him in daily bread,
while he mourns for his mannerly verses
that had left so much unsaid.

LOUIS MACNEICE 1907-1963

Prayer Before Birth

I am not yet born; O hear me.
Let not the bloodsucking bat or the rat or the stoat or the
    club-footed ghoul come near me.

I am not yet born, console me.
I fear that the human race may with tall walls wall me,
    with strong drugs dope me, with wise lies lure me,
      on black racks rack me, in blood-baths roll me.

I am not yet born; provide me
With water to dandle me, grass to grow for me, trees to talk
    to me, sky to sing to me, birds and a white light
      in the back of my mind to guide me.

I am not yet born; forgive me
For the sins that in me the world shall commit, my words
    when they speak me, my thoughts when they think me,
      my treason engendered by traitors beyond me,
        my life when they murder by means of my
          hands, my death when they live me.

I am not yet born; rehearse me
In the parts I must play and the cues I must take when
    old men lecture me, bureaucrats hector me, mountains
      frown at me, lovers laugh at me, the white
        waves call me to folly and the desert calls
          me to doom and the beggar refuses
            my gift and my children curse me.

I am not yet born; O hear me,
Let not the man who is beast or who thinks he is God
    come near me.

I am not yet born; O fill me
With strength against those who would freeze my
    humanity, would dragoon me into a lethal automaton,
      would make me a cog in a machine, a thing with
        one face, a thing, and against all those

who would dissipate my entirety, would
blow me like thistledown hither and
thither or hither and thither
like water held in the
hands would spill me.

Let them not make me a stone and let them not spill me.
Otherwise kill me.

Carrickfergus

I was born in Belfast between the mountain and the gantries
  To the hooting of lost sirens and the clang of trams:
Thence to Smoky Carrick in County Antrim
  Where the bottle-neck harbour collects the mud which jams

The little boats beneath the Norman castle,
  The pier shining with lumps of crystal salt;
The Scotch Quarter was a line of residential houses
  But the Irish Quarter was a slum for the blind and halt.

The brook ran yellow from the factory stinking of chlorine,
  The yarn-mill called its funeral cry at noon;
Our lights looked over the lough to the lights of Bangor
  Under the peacock aura of a drowning moon.

The Norman walled this town against the country
  To stop his ears to the yelping of his slave
And built a church in the form of a cross but denoting
  The list of Christ on the cross in the angle of the nave.

I was the rector's son, born to the anglican order,
    Banned for ever from the candles of the Irish poor;
The Chichesters knelt in marble at the end of a transept
    With ruffs about their necks, their portion sure.

The war came and a huge camp of soldiers
    Grew from the ground in sight of our house with long
Dummies hanging from gibbets for bayonet practice
    And the sentry's challenge echoing all day long;

A Yorkshire terrier ran in and out by the gate-lodge
    Barred to civilians, yapping as if taking affront:
Marching at ease and singing 'Who Killed Cock Robin?'
    The troops went out by the lodge and off to the Front.

The steamer was camouflaged that took me to England—
    Sweat and khaki in the Carlisle train;
I thought that the war would last for ever and sugar
    Be always rationed and that never again

Would the weekly papers not have photos of sandbags
    And my governess not make bandages from moss
And people not have maps above the fireplace
    With flags on pins moving across and across—

Across the hawthorn hedge the noise of bugles,
    Flares across the night,
Somewhere on the lough was a prison ship for Germans,
    A cage across their sight.

I went to school in Dorset, the world of parents
    Contracted into a puppet world of sons
Far from the mill girls, the smell of porter, the salt-mines
    And the soldiers with their guns.

Autobiography

In my childhood trees were green
And there was plenty to be seen.

Come back early or never come.

My father made the walls resound,
He wore his collar the wrong way round.

Come back early or never come.

My mother wore a yellow dress;
Gentle, gently, gentleness.

Come back early or never come.

When I was five the black dreams came;
Nothing after was quite the same.

Come back early or never come.

The dark was talking to the dead;
The lamp was dark beside my bed.

Come back early or never come.

When I woke they did not care;
Nobody, nobody was there.

Come back early or never come.

When my silent terror cried,
Nobody, nobody replied.

Come back early or never come.

I got up; the chilly sun
Saw me walk away alone.

Come back early or never come.

When We Were Children

When we were children words were coloured
(Harlot and murder were dark purple)
And language was a prism, the light
    A conjured inlay on the grass,
Whose rays today are concentrated
    And language grown a burning-glass.

When we were children Spring was easy,
Dousing our heads in suds of hawthorn
And scrambling the laburnum tree—
    A breakfast for the gluttonous eye;
Whose winds and sweets have now forsaken
    Lungs that are black, tongues that are dry.

Now we are older and our talents
Accredited to time and meaning,
To handsel joy requires a new
    Shuffle of cards behind the brain
Where meaning shall remarry colour
    And flowers be timeless once again.

Sunday Morning

Down the road someone is practising scales,
The notes like little fishes vanish with a wink of tails,
Man's heart expands to tinker with his car
For this is Sunday morning, Fate's great bazaar;
Regard these means as ends, concentrate on this Now,
And you may grow to music or drive beyond Hindhead anyhow,
Take corners on two wheels until you go so fast
That you can clutch a fringe or two of the windy past,
That you can abstract this day and make it to the week of time
A small eternity, a sonnet self-contained in rhyme.

But listen, up the road, something gulps, the church spire
Opens its eight bells out, skulls' mouths which will not tire
To tell how there is no music or movement which secures
Escape from the weekday time. Which deadens and endures.

Snow

The room was suddenly rich and the great bay-window was
Spawning snow and pink roses against it
Soundlessly collateral and incompatible:
World is suddener than we fancy it.

World is crazier and more of it than we think,
Incorrigibly plural. I peel and portion
A tangerine and spit the pips and feel
The drunkenness of things being various.

And the fire flames with a bubbling sound for world
Is more spiteful and gay than one supposes—
On the tongue on the eyes on the ears in the palms of one's
    hands—
There is more than glass between the snow and the huge roses.

Death of an Old Lady

At five in the morning there were grey voices
Calling three times through the dank fields;
The ground fell away beyond the voices
Forty long years to the wrinkled lough
That had given a child one shining glimpse
Of a boat so big it was named Titanic.

Named or called? For a name is a call—
Shipyard voices at five in the morning,
As now for this old tired lady who sails
Towards her own iceberg calm and slow;
We hardly hear the screws, we hardly
Can think her back her four score years.

They called and ceased. Later the night nurse
Handed over, the day went down
To the sea in a ship, it was grey April,
The daffodils in her garden waited
To make her a wreath, the iceberg waited;
At eight in the evening the ship went down.

Death of an Actress

I see from the paper that Florrie Forde is dead—
Collapsed after singing to wounded soldiers,
At the age of sixty-five. The American notice
Says no doubt all that need be said

About this one-time chorus girl; whose rôle
For more than forty stifling years was giving
Sexual, sentimental, or comic entertainment,
A gaudy posy for the popular soul.

Plush and cigars: she waddled into the lights,
Old and huge and painted, in velvet and tiara,
Her voice gone but around her head an aura
Of all her vanilla-sweet forgotten vaudeville nights.

With an elephantine shimmy and a sugared wink
She threw a trellis of Dorothy Perkins roses
Around an audience come from slum and suburb
And weary of the tea-leaves in the sink;

Who found her songs a rainbow leading west
To the home they never had, to the chocolate Sunday
Of boy and girl, to cowslip time, to the never-
Ending weekend Islands of the Blest.

In the Isle of Man before the war before
The present one she made a ragtime favourite
Of 'Tipperary', which became the swan-song
Of troop-ships on a darkened shore;

And during Munich sang her ancient quiz
Of *Where's Bill Bailey?* and the chorus answered,
Muddling through and glad to have no answer:
Where's Bill Bailey? How do *we* know where he is!

Now on a late and bandaged April day
In a military hospital Miss Florrie
Forde has made her positively last appearance
And taken her bow and gone correctly away.

Correctly. For she stood
For an older England, for children toddling
Hand in hand while the day was bright. Let the wren and robin
Gently with leaves cover the Babes in the Wood.

Bagpipe Music

It's no go the merrygoround, it's no go the rickshaw,
All we want is a limousine and a ticket for the peepshow.
Their knickers are made of crêpe-de-chine, their shoes are made of
      python,
Their halls are lined with tiger rugs and their walls with heads of
      bison.

John MacDonald found a corpse, put it under the sofa,
Waited till it came to life and hit it with a poker,
Sold its eyes for souvenirs, sold its blood for whiskey,
Kept its bones for dumb-bells to use when he was fifty.

It's no go the Yogi-Man, it's no go Blavatsky,
All we want is a bank balance and a bit of skirt in a taxi.

Annie MacDougall went to milk, caught her foot in the heather,
Woke to hear a dance record playing of Old Vienna.
It's no go your maidenheads, it's no go your culture,
All we want is a Dunlop tyre and the devil mend the puncture.

The Laird o' Phelps spent Hogmanay declaring he was sober,
Counted his feet to prove the fact and found he had one foot over.
Mrs. Carmichael had her fifth, looked at the job with repulsion,
Said to the midwife, 'Take it away; I'm through with over-
      production.'

It's no go the gossip column, it's no go the Ceilidh,
All we want is a mother's help and a sugar-stick for the baby.

Willie Murray cut his thumb, couldn't count the damage,
Took the hide of an Ayrshire cow and used it for a bandage.
His brother caught three hundred cran when the seas were lavish,
Threw the bleeders back in the sea and went upon the parish.

It's no go the Herring Board, it's no go the Bible,
All we want is a packet of fags when our hands are idle.

It's no go the picture palace, it's no go the stadium,
It's no go the country cot with a pot of pink geraniums,
It's no go the Government grants, it's no go the elections,
Sit on your arse for fifty years and hang your hat on a pension.

It's no go my honey love, it's no go my poppet;
Work your hands from day to day, the winds will blow the profit.
The glass is falling hour by hour, the glass will fall for ever,
But if you break the bloody glass you won't hold up the weather.

Conversation

Ordinary people are peculiar too:
Watch the vagrant in their eyes
Who sneaks away while they are talking with you
Into some black wood behind the skull,
Following un-, or other, realities,
Fishing for shadows in a pool.

But sometimes the vagrant comes the other way
Out of their eyes and into yours
Having mistaken you perhaps for yesterday
Or for to-morrow night, a wood in which
He may pick up among the pine-needles and burrs
The lost purse, the dropped stitch.

Vagrancy however is forbidden; ordinary men
Soon come back to normal, look you straight
In the eyes as if to say 'It will not happen again',
Put up a barrage of common sense to baulk
Intimacy but by mistake interpolate
Swear-words like roses in their talk.

Coda

Maybe we knew each other better
When the night was young and unrepeated
And the moon stood still over Jericho.

So much for the past; in the present
There are moments caught between heart-beats
When maybe we know each other better.

But what is that clinking in the darkness?
Maybe we shall know each other better
When the tunnels meet beneath the mountain.

The Sunlight on the Garden

The sunlight on the garden
Hardens and grows cold,
We cannot cage the minute
Within its nets of gold,
When all is told
We cannot beg for pardon.

Our freedom as free-lances
Advances towards its end;
The earth compels, upon it
Sonnets and birds descend;
And soon, my friend,
We shall have no time for dances.

The sky was good for flying
Defying the church bells
And every evil iron
Siren and what it tells:
The earth compels,
We are dying, Egypt, dying

And not expecting pardon,
Hardened in heart anew,
But glad to have sat under
Thunder and rain with you,
And grateful too
For sunlight on the garden.

Meeting-Point

Time was away and somewhere else,
There were two glasses and two chairs
And two people with the one pulse
(Somebody stopped the moving stairs):
Time was away and somewhere else.

And they were neither up nor down;
The stream's music did not stop
Flowing through heather, limpid brown,
Although they sat in a coffee shop
And they were neither up nor down.

The bell was silent in the air
Holding its inverted poise—
Between the clang and clang a flower,
A brazen calyx of no noise:
The bell was silent in the air.

The camels crossed the miles of sand
That stretched around the cups and plates;
The desert was their own, they planned
To portion out the stars and dates:
The camels crossed the miles of sand.

Time was away and somewhere else.
The waiter did not come, the clock
Forgot them and the radio waltz
Came out like water from a rock:
Time was away and somewhere else.

Her fingers flicked away the ash
That bloomed again in tropic trees:
Not caring if the markets crash
When they had forests such as these,
Her fingers flicked away the ash.

God or whatever means the Good
Be praised that time can stop like this,
That what the heart has understood
Can verify in the body's peace
God or whatever means the Good.

Time was away and she was here
And life no longer what it was,
The bell was silent in the air
And all the room one glow because
Time was away and she was here.

The Introduction

They were introduced in a grave glade
And she frightened him because she was young
And thus too late. Crawly crawly
Went the twigs above their heads and beneath
The grass beneath their feet the larvae
Split themselves laughing. Crawly crawly
Went the cloud above the treetops reaching
For a sun that lacked the nerve to set

And he frightened her because he was old
And thus too early. Crawly crawly
Went the string quartet that was tuning up
In the back of the mind. You two should have met
Long since, he said, or else not now.
The string quartet in the back of the mind
Was all tuned up with nowhere to go.
They were introduced in a green grave.

Night-Club

After the legshows and the brandies
And all the pick-me-ups for tired
Men there is a feeling
Something more is required.

The lights go down and eyes
Look up across the room;
Salome comes in, bearing
The head of God knows whom.

Entirely

If we could get the hang of it entirely
    It would take too long;
All we know is the splash of words in passing
    And falling twigs of song,
And when we try to eavesdrop on the great
    Presences it is rarely

That by a stroke of luck we can appropriate
   Even a phrase entirely.

If we could find our happiness entirely
   In somebody else's arms
We should not fear the spears of the spring nor the city's
   Yammering fire alarms
But, as it is, the spears each year go through
   Our flesh and almost hourly
Bell or siren banishes the blue
   Eyes of Love entirely.

And if the world were black or white entirely
   And all the charts were plain
Instead of a mad weir of tigerish waters,
   A prism of delight and pain,
We might be surer where we wished to go
   Or again we might be merely
Bored but in brute reality there is no
   Road that is right entirely.

The Truisms

His father gave him a box of truisms
Shaped like a coffin, then his father died;
The truisms remained on the mantelpiece
As wooden as the playbox they had been packed in
Or that other his father skulked inside.

Then he left home, left the truisms behind him
Still on the mantelpiece, met love, met war,
Sordor, disappointment, defeat, betrayal,
Till through disbeliefs he arrived at a house
He could not remember seeing before,

And he walked straight in; it was where he had come from
And something told him the way to behave.
He raised his hand and blessed his home;
The truisms flew and perched on his shoulders
And a tall tree sprouted from his father's grave.

The Taxis

In the first taxi he was alone tra-la,
No extras on the clock. He tipped ninepence
But the cabby, while he thanked him, looked askance
As though to suggest someone had bummed a ride.

In the second taxi he was alone tra-la
But the clock showed sixpence extra; he tipped according
And the cabby from out of his muffler said: 'Make sure
You have left nothing behind tra-la between you'.

In the third taxi he was alone tra-la
But the tip-up seats were down and there was an extra
Charge of one-and-sixpence and an odd
Scent that reminded him of a trip to Cannes.

As for the fourth taxi, he was alone
Tra-la when he hailed it but the cabby looked
Through him and said: 'I can't tra-la well take
So many people, not to speak of the dog.'

Charon

The conductor's hands were black with money:
Hold on to your ticket, he said, the inspector's
Mind is black with suspicion, and hold on to
That dissolving map. We moved through London,
We could see the pigeons through the glass but failed
To hear their rumours of wars, we could see
The lost dog barking but never knew
That his bark was as shrill as a cock crowing,
We just jogged on, at each request
Stop there was a crowd of aggressively vacant
Faces, we just jogged on, eternity
Gave itself airs in revolving lights
And then we came to the Thames and all
The bridges were down, the further shore
Was lost in fog, so we asked the conductor
What we should do. He said: Take the ferry
Faute de mieux. We flicked the flashlight
And there was the ferryman just as Virgil
And Dante had seen him. He looked at us coldly
And his eyes were dead and his hands on the oar
Were black with obols and varicose veins
Marbled his calves and he said to us coldly:
If you want to die you will have to pay for it.

Thalassa

Run out the boat, my broken comrades;
Let the old seaweed crack, the surge
Burgeon oblivious of the last
Embarkation of feckless men,
Let every adverse force converge—
Here we must needs embark again.

Run up the sail, my heartsick comrades;
Let each horizon tilt and lurch—
You know the worst: your wills are fickle,
Your values blurred, your hearts impure
And your past life a ruined church—
But let your poison be your cure.

Put out to sea, ignoble comrades,
Whose record shall be noble yet;
Butting through scarps of moving marble
The narwhal dares us to be free;
By a high star our course is set,
Our end is Life. Put out to sea.

W R RODGERS 1909-1969

Words

Always the arriving winds of words
Pour like Atlantic gales over these ears,
These reefs, these foils and fenders, these shrinking
And sea-scalded edges of the brain-land.
Rebutted and rebounding, on they post
Past my remembrance, falling all unplanned.
But some day out of darkness they'll come forth,
Arrowed and narrowed into my tongue's tip,
And speak for me—their most astonished host.

The Lovers

After the tiff there was stiff silence, till
One word, flung in centre like single stone,
Starred and cracked the ice of her resentment
To its edge. From that stung core opened and
Poured up one outward and widening wave
Of eager and extravagant anger.

Stormy Night

Is this the street? Never a sign of life,
The swinging lamp throws everything about;
But see! from that sly doorway, like a knife
The gilt edge of inviting light slides out
And in again—the very sign
Of her whose slightest nod I lately thought was mine;

But not now.
Knock! and the night-flowering lady
Opens, and across the brilliant sill
Sees me standing there so dark and shady
Hugging the silences of my ill-will;
Wildly she turns from me—But no, my love,
This foot's within the door, this hand's without the glove.

Well may you tremble now, and say there was nothing meant,
And curl away from my care with a 'Please, my dear!',
For though you were smoke, sucked up by a raging vent,
I'd follow you through every flue of your fear,
And over your faraway arms I'll mountain and cone
In a pillar of carolling fire and fountaining stone.

O strike the gong of your wrong, raise the roof of your rage,
Fist and foist me off with a cloud of cries,
What do I care for all your footling rampage?
On your light-in-gale blows my larking caresses will rise,
But—Why so still? What! are you weeping, my sweet?
Ah heart, heart, look! I throw myself at your feet.

The Net

Quick, woman, in your net
Catch the silver I fling!
O I am deep in your debt,
Draw tight, skin-tight, the string,
And rake the silver in.
No fisher ever yet
Drew such a cunning ring.

Ah, shifty as the fin
Of any fish this flesh
That, shaken to the shin,
Now shoals into your mesh,
Bursting to be held in;
Purse-proud and pebble-hard,
Its pence like shingle showered.

Open the haul, and shake
The fill of shillings free,
Let all the satchels break
And leap about the knee
In shoals of ecstasy.
Guineas and gills will flake
At each gull-plunge of me.

Though all the Angels, and
Saint Michael at their head,
Nightly contrive to stand
On guard about your bed,
Yet none dare take a hand,
But each can only spread
His eagle-eye instead.

But I, being man, can kiss
And bed-spread-eagle too;
All flesh shall come to this,
Being less than angel is,
Yet higher far in bliss
As it entwines with you.

Come, make no sound, my sweet;
Turn down the candid lamp
And draw the equal quilt
Over our naked guilt.

Lent

Mary Magdalene, that easy woman,
Saw, from the shore, the seas
Beat against the hard stone of Lent,
Crying, 'Weep, seas, weep
For yourselves that cannot dent me more.

O more than all these, more crabbed than all stones,
And cold, make me, who once
Could leap like water, Lord. Take me
As one who owes
Nothing to what she was. Ah, naked.

My waves of scent, my petticoats of foam
Put from me and rebut;
Disown. And that salt lust stave off
That slavered me—O
Let it whiten in grief against the stones

And outer reefs of me. Utterly doff,
Nor leave the lightest veil
Of feeling to heave or soften.
Nothing cares this heart
What hardness crates it now or coffins.

Over the balconies of these curved breasts
I'll no more peep to see
The light procession of my loves
Surf-riding in to me
Who now have eyes and alcove, Lord, for Thee.'

'Room, Mary,' said He, 'ah make room for me
Who am come so cold now
To my tomb.' So, on Good Friday,
Under a frosty moon
They carried Him and laid Him in her womb.

A grave and icy mask her heart wore twice,
But on the third day it thawed,
And only a stone's-flow away
Mary saw her God.
Did you hear me? Mary saw her God!

Dance, Mary Magdalene, dance, dance and sing,
For unto you is born
This day a King. 'Lady,' said He,
'To you who relent
I bring back the petticoat and the bottle of scent.'

The Swan

Bottomed by tugging combs of water
The slow and loath swan slews and looks
Coldly down through chutes of stilled chatter
Upon the shadows in flight among the stones.

Into abashed confusions of ooze
It dips, and from the muddy fume
The silver and flute-like fishes rise
Endlessly up through all their octaves of gloom

To where the roofed swan suavely swings
Without qualm on the quivering wave
That laves it on, with elbowing wings held wide
Under its eyes' hugged look and architrave.

Jonquil-long its neck adjudicates
Its body's course; aloof and cool
It cons the nonchalant and unseeing air
With its incurious and dispassionate stare.

Slow, slow, it slides, as if not to chafe
The even sleeve of its approach
Stretched stiff and oval in front of it,
Siphoning it on, selfless, silent, and safe.

On that grey lake, frilled round with scufflings
Of foam and milled with muttering
I saw lingering, late and lightless,
A single swan, swinging, sleek as a sequin.

Negligently bright, wide wings pinned back,
It mooned on the moving water,
And not all the close and gartering dark
Or gathering wind could lift or flatter
That small and dimming image into flight;
Far from shore and free from foresight,
Coiled in its own indifferent mood
It held the heavens, shores, waters and all their brood.

The Party

So they went, leaving a picnic-litter of talk
And broken glitter of jokes, the burst bags of spite:
In comes Contempt the caretaker, eye on ceiling,
Broom in armpit, and with one wide careless cast
Sweeps the stuttering rubbish out of memory,
Opens the shutters, puts out the intimate lamp,
And, a moment, gazes on the mute enormities
Of distant dawn. And far doors bang in mind, idly.

from Resurrection: an Easter Sequence

Then cometh Jesus with them unto a place called Gethsemane.

It was a lovely night,
A night for weddings and for water.
Going out into the cold glow he felt washed
And clean of people. The garden had an air
Of waiting about it, as if the leaves were bent
On eavesdropping. And the rain
Scented the air with more-than-midnight pain
And the wet trees that had nowhere to go
Stood round and gazed at the One walking there below
In agony. Ebb and flow, to and fro, Yes and No;
Doubt assailed him. Which and what to do? This much must be
    admitted,
We live between two worlds, faith and doubt,
Like breath. The air that one breathes does not care
Whether it's in or out; it's not in love with life
Or death. And yet we do not dare to hold it long,
But must let go to find again. So with faith,
With love, with everything. Now at the cross-roads,
Middled and muddled he stood.
This was it. And it was night. 'Nevertheless Thy will be done.'
That thought made morning of it, gave him ease, and issue.
He knew now how to stay and stare it out
And already the torches approached the garden.

And when he had scourged Jesus, he delivered him to be crucified.

They took him out to die.
The lark was shaking out its acres of song in the sky
And the sun shone. People looked up and remarked
What a wonderful day it was going to be
And the cheering boys ran on in front of the crowd,
And the cheeky ones waited to stare.
                        Once he noticed
A blind man whom he had healed looking at him

With horrified eyes as much as to say
'Was it for this I was given sight by the god that day?'
He turned away. If only this had been an important death,
If only he knew that the people who barracked him now
Had been travelling years and years to reach this place.
But they were casual passers-by and their interest was jaded.
Yet it was all as he had expected, and
He would not avoid or evade it. Far away
A spool of birds was spinning above the hill,
And still Pilate sat in the empty court beneath,
Sucking threads of thoughtfulness through his teeth.

And they crucified him.

This was a rough death, there was nothing tidy about it,
No sweetness, nothing noble.
Everything stuck out awkwardly and angular:
The clumsy soldier brought the wrong basket of nails;
And the couriers—those sticky fly-papers of events—
Did not even bother to cover his sticky end,
Or carry it home to Rome. For them the war in Gaul
Was more important; the ship of state sailed on,
Leaving him bogging in the backward seas.
Still, that is how things always happen, lousily,
But later on, the heart edits them lovingly,
Abstracts the jeers and jags, imports a plan
Into the pain, and calls it history.
We always go back to gloss over some roughness,
To make the past happen properly as we want it to happen.
But this was a hard death. At the time
There was no room for thought.
How often he had hearsed and rehearsed this hour.
But when you come up against it all the good words about it
Are less than breath. It is hard to turn the other cheek
When both have been slapped:
                    Yes, it was a hard death.

Now there stood by the Cross of Jesus his mother...

A mist opened and closed its eyes before him,
And in it he saw her looking at him
The untouchable terrible god.
O what ladders of longing led up from her
To him, what steps and depths of memory ran down;
He remembered the happy days in Galilee
When he was heaven's hub; the heap of smoking grass,
The bubble-pipe, the light upon the wall,
The children in the far garden looking for the lost ball,
And Mary calling him. He was always so distant
In those lonely days. O if only
He had mattered less, she wondered, if only
She had mastered him more, would he then
Have been like other men, a flat satisfied plain?
But no. In him mountains of onlyness rose
Snow-high. Dayspring was in his eyes
At midnight. And he would not come down
From his far purpose even for her who was
The root that raised him to this Cross and crown
Of thorns. Yet tenderly he spoke
Goodbye now, his voice choking and dry.
And as she went away, leaving him to die,
The vast moon of his cry rose up upon the darkness.
His heart broke.

And there was Mary Magdalene and the other Mary, sitting over
against the sepulchre...

It is always the women who are the Watchers
And keepers of life: they guard our exits
And our entrances. They are both tomb and womb,
End and beginning. Bitterly they bring forth
And bitterly take back the light they gave.
The last to leave and still the first to come,

They circle us like sleep or like the grave.
Earth is their element, and in it lies
The seed and silence of the lighted skies,
The seasons with their fall and slow uprise,
Man with his sight and militant surmise.
It is always the women who are the Watchers
And Wakeners.

Field Day

The old farmer, nearing death, asked
To be carried outside and set down
Where he could see a certain field
'And then I will cry my heart out,' he said.

It troubles me, thinking about that man;
What shape was the field of his crying
In Donegal?

I remember a small field in Down, a field
Within fields, shaped like a triangle.
I could have stood there and looked at it
All day long.

And I remember crossing the frontier between
France and Spain at a forbidden point, and seeing
A small triangular field in Spain,
And stopping

Or walking in Ireland down any rutted by-road
To where it hit the highway, there was always
At this turning-point and abutment
A still centre, a V-shape of grass
Untouched by cornering traffic,
Where country lads larked at night.

I think I know what the shape of the field was
That made the old man weep.

ROY McFADDEN b. 1921

Epithalamium

So you are married, girl. It makes me sad
At heart to think that you, last summer held
Between hot hands on slow white afternoons,
Whose eyes I knew down to their blackest depths,
(Stirred by the indolent smile and the quick laugh)
Are married now. Some man whom I have not seen
Calls up the smile and the laugh, holds in his hands
The welcoming body, sees in the darkening eyes
Sufficient future in a shaded room.
I wish you well. Now, with twin-set and pearls,
Your girlhood gone, that summer on your skin,
You'll settle down, keep up appearances.
I, wed to history, pray for your peace;
That the smile be never twisted in your mouth,
And the pond of your mind never be rippled with sorrow:
That you may sleep your sleep as the world quakes,
And never see the chasms at your feet.

from Memories of Chinatown

Bigamy

His cycle kerbed, the peeler found
The lad behind the door, the girl
Biting her flowered pinafore,
Hushed neighbours aching for a sound.

He went off with the constable,
Cap wedged inside his pocket with
A blackened butt and one red match,
And helped to push the bicycle.

The girl stole in and closed the blinds.
Neighbours stormed to angry pans
And urgent irons' climbing steam,
Straitlaced within their marriage-lines.

But no one chased the constable
To ask what harm the lad had done
In kindling love on her cold hearth;
Or who would be accountable

For her trousseau of cast-off love,
Her honeymoon arrested; shame
Shrouding her presence like a shawl,
Bare thumb betrayed by Sunday glove.

Contemplations of Mary

1

When he said *Mary*, she did not at once
Look up to find the voice, but sat recalling
Warm patches of her childhood, and her falling
Heartoverhead in love with every glance
Of admiration crowding through the dance,
Or in the streets bent back and almost calling.

Girls put on sex like flowers; their small breasts
Emerge like blushes, knowing, innocent;
The underflow of all their ways intent
On welling up with welcome for the guests
Who darken love's white threshold. All the rest's
Above, outside, like god and government.

So she sat on when he first spoke to her.
Hearing perhaps a new sound of command,
Like parent's tug at child's reluctant hand,
Did not at once look up and answer *Sir*,
But sat with memory her conspirator,
Downcast, and did not want to understand.

But he persisted. *Mary*. She resigned
Her meadows and her rainbows to his voice,
Inevitably now, without a choice,
Surrendering all the stairways of her mind;
Then, finally bereft, was empty, blind,
Until the word bulged up and broke. *Rejoice*.

2

Then she was different. Her past perfect years
Seemed like another woman's purse, all strange
In ordinary things, keys, compact, change:
And home no longer nested up those stairs,
Involved with tables, pictures, cupboards, chairs.

Everything was leaning out askew
Since it had touched, no hardly touched her, blown
A strange breath through her branches and the mown
And planted garden of her private view,
Those yesterdays no longer *I* but *you*.

Was it her knowledge of the clouded womb
That crowded out her quiet corridors:
Her certainty of child? Or, like far doors
Slamming goodbyes, was it a shout of doom,
The dying of a world in her small room:

Her mind a skirt of fear ballooning back
To girlish unencumbered days when life
Required no definitions; sweetheart, wife
Made love, embroidered, lived without some lack
Of meaning like a rat at every crack:

Mary, still girl enough to twirl her hood
From birth and death conspiring in her blood
Against the bright truth of her platitude?

3

After the dying, tidying her room,
She pondered, wondered why he had cried out
In protest for his father. Was his shout
Indictment of the seed that filled her womb
Or plea for some known name to mark his tomb?
Now she was parched and hollowed out with doubt.

She had been satisfied the way things were,
Girl among girls, doing the usual things.
Then she had been exalted, hearing wings
Applauding through the galleries of air;
Came to know words that first had made her stare,
And talk to common people as to kings.

It never was her doing. She had been
Only the bottle for the conjured wine.
Involved with something magic or divine,
She had no axe to grind, no slate to clean,
Had never bothered with a party line.
Most of the things he said she did not mean.

Now she was empty. The last drop had gone,
And she was her own Mary, uninvolved
With parables or politics, resolved
To self, undedicated, pledged to none.
And just before the colours blurred, dissolved,
She closed the door on her disfigured son.

4

I am the breath that stirred
Your bells to jubilance;
Conjured from cold distance
As surely as a bird
Immense obeisance:
I am the word.

My irresponsible
Dialogue broke down,
Was hooted, hissed and blown
Off stage in ridicule,
My sad forgiving clown
A love-crossed fool.

But I would blow again
My horn into your sleep;
Herd rational thought like sheep
Into a nursery pen;
Scatter my wolves to sweep
Doubt from the plain.

Yes, I would fill your page,
Your lines with poetry:
With liberating key
Empty the clipped lark's cage,
And give back wings to free
Ecstatic rage.

Mary, I am cold,
Bare on the brink of mind.
Open, and let me find
A place to grip and hold,
To thrust the exiled seed
In knowing mould.

First Letter to an Irish Novelist
for Michael McLaverty

Establishment has taken to the hills.
The capitals are bombed. But you pursue
Survival in minute particulars,
Your landscapes, intimate with sea and sky,
Perpetual, unblemished idiom
Common as dolmens and the Easter whin.

Even this city reveals dignity,
Turning a startled face from history.
If you ignore the adolescent dream,
The club-fists of the mob, the tumbled bed,
It is because, the final pattern known,
You choose the threads. And local hatreds fail
To churn your vistas into stony grass,
Or drown you in a puddle's politics.

Chance friendships are not always fortunate.
I think of someone, mutually known,
Complacent as a throstle bosoming song
Above the matchstick silhouetted town
Caught in the headlights of advancing war;
And of another portly pedant who
Talks of the revolution from a chair,
Stroking his stomach; and of that old man
Walking in mountains, gnarled with stern regret
At missing greatness (the erratic bus).

And then I think of Ireland. Of blue roads
That rivulet into Aeonic seas;
The fields bogged down with failure; the downfall
Of honest men perverted by a cause
Or dangerous verses irresponsibly
Let loose by poets, and adopted by
The semi-literate candidates for power,
Or turned to dogma in schoolchildren's mouths.

Those who have lost a country, with a wound
In place of patria, can sail like winds
Among the islands and the continents,
Flying, if any, only personal flags,
Educated to brave devious seas,
Sceptical of harbours, fortunate
In being themselves, each with his personal war.

And they have charts and compasses, for some
Have made the voyage out before their time,
Confronting tempests, fangs of submarines,
Alerted to the coasts' hostility,
The accents foreign and the flags suspect.
A few received an ocean burial,
Having lost sight of continents too long,
Crazed by a magnitude of space and time,
Agnostic salt in the nostalgic wound.

We shall be wary then, and weatherwise,
Testing our strength of sail, learning the ways
Of sinuous currents singing in the rocks,
And the exotic dreams that come from thirst
And too much loneliness on the world's edge,
The fear of mutiny and the dark hold,
The shark's fin in the wave, the loitering mines.

In time the navigator holds a course,
And heads for landfall. Yes; but, you'll observe,
The missions follow, organised with flags
And bibles for the natives. Be assured
The paths and footholds left by us will fill
With vendors of a new conformity,
Briefed by accountants. Turn to the running sea,
That carries shells like mouths to the hushed sand.

Stringer's Field

This is no proper route for middle-age
Seeking the stirrups of a rocking horse,
Key lacking door, superior car too big
For the meagre streets of Kick-the-can and Tig.

I have gone back too far. Then a townland,
Before the first death, brimmed and hummed
    with summer,
And life like loafing kerbstones stretched eternal
And The News was always the same from wireless
    and journal.

I have gone back too far. Then that white summer
Trite with daisies and the next-door girl's
Buttercup kiss through the laurels when we were seven,
And at night the streetlamp guttering up to heaven,

My robining boyhood under Stringer's trees:
Now, leafed back, reveals the kerbstones cold,
Kiss blown, ironic laurels unallayed
By my return to all I left unsaid.

PADRAIC FIACC b. 1924

Gloss

Nor truth nor good did they know
But beauty burning away.

They were the dark earth people
                            of old
Restive in the clay...

Deirdre watched Naisi die
And great King Conor of himself
                            said

'Did you ever see a bottomless
                            bucket
In the muck discarded?'

And comradely Dermot was destroyed by Fionn

Because of the beauty of a girl.

Because of the beauty of a girl
The sky went raging on fire

And the sea was pushed out into
                            rage.

They were the dark earth people
                            of old

And Deirdre pitched herself into
                            the sea.
Turn the page. Turn the page.

First Movement

for Alan Rodgers

Low clouds yellow in a mist wind
Sift on far-off ards
Drift hazily...

I was born on such a morning
Smelling of the Bone Yards

The smoking chimneys over
                    the slate roof-tops
The wayward storm birds

And to the east where morning is
                    the sea
And to the west where evening is
                    the sea
Threatening with danger
                    and it
Would always darken suddenly.

Soldiers

for Seamus Deane

The altar boy marches up the altar steps.
The priest marches down. 'Get up now
And be a soldier!' says the nun
To the woman after giving birth, 'Get up now
And march, march: Be a man!'

And the men are men and the women are men
And the children are men!

Mother carried a knife to work.
It was the thorn to her rose...

They say she died with her eyes open
In the French Hospital in New York.
I remember those eyes shining in the dark

Slum hallway the day after
I left the monastery: Eyes that were
A feast of welcome that said 'Yes,
I'm glad you didn't stay stuck there!'

'Would you mind if I went to prison
Rather than war?'
'No, for Ireland's men all went to prison!'

At the bottom of a canyon of brick
She cursed and swore
'You never see the sky!'

A lifetime after
                    just before
I go to sleep at night, I hear
That Anna Magnani voice screaming
Me deaf 'No! No, you're not
To heed the world!' In one swift
Sentence she tells me not to yield
But to *forbear*:
                    'Go to prison but never
Never stop fighting. We are the poor
And the poor have to be "soldiers".

You're still a soldier, it's only that
You're losing the war

And all the wars are lost anyway!'

Enemy Encounter

for Lilac

Dumping (left over from the autumn)
Dead leaves, near a culvert
I come on
                    a British Army Soldier
With a rifle and a radio
Perched hiding. He has red hair.

He is young enough to be my weenie
-bopper daughter's boy-friend.
He is like a lonely little winter robin.

We are that close to each other, I
Can nearly hear his heart beating.

I say something bland to make him grin,
But his glass eyes look past my side
-whiskers down
                    the Shore Road street.
I am an Irish man
                    and he is afraid
That I have come to kill him.

Saint Coleman's Song for Flight

for Nancy and Brigid—flown

Run like rats from the plague in you.
Before death it is no virtue to be dead.
The crannog in the water, anywhere at all sure!
It is no virtue and it is not nature
To wait to writhe into the ground.

Not one in the Bible could see these dead
Packed on top of the other like dung
Not the two Josephs in Egypt
But would not run!

And Christ's blessing follow
(Is it not a blessing to escape storm?)

Pray to old Joseph not a witless man
Who had the brains not to want to die

But when his time came only and at home in bed,
The door shut on the world, that wolf outside
Munching the leper's head...

JOHN MONTAGUE b. 1929

Like Dolmens Round My Childhood, the Old People

Like dolmens round my childhood, the old people.

Jamie MacCrystal sang to himself
A broken song, without tune, without words;
He tipped me a penny every pension day,
Fed kindly crusts to winter birds.
When he died his cottage was robbed,
Mattress and money box torn and searched,
Only the corpse they didn't disturb.

Maggie Owens was surrounded by animals,
A mongrel bitch and shivering pups,
Even in her bedroom a she-goat cried,
She was a well of gossip defiled,
Fanged chronicler of a whole countryside;
Reputed a witch, all I could find
Was her lonely need to deride.

The Nialls lived along a mountain lane
Where heather bells bloomed, clumps of foxglove.
All were blind, with Blind Pension and Wireless.
Dead eyes serpent-flickered as one entered
To shelter from a downpour of mountain rain.
Crickets chirped under the rocking hearthstone
Until the muddy sun shone out again.

Mary Moore lived in a crumbling gatehouse
Famous as Pisa for its leaning gable.
Bag apron and boots, she tramped the fields
Driving lean cattle to a miry stable.
A by-word for fierceness, she fell asleep
Over love stories, Red Star and Red Circle,
Dreamed of gypsy love rites, by firelight sealed.

Wild Billy Harbinson married a Catholic servant girl
When all his loyal family passed on:
We danced round him shouting 'To hell with King Billy'

And dodged from the arc of his flailing blackthorn.
Forsaken by both creeds, he showed little concern
Until the Orange drums banged past in the summer
And bowler and sash aggressively shone.

Curate and doctor trudged to attend them,
Through knee-deep snow, through summer heat,
From main road to lane to broken path,
Gulping the mountain air with painful breath.
Sometimes they were found by neighbours,
Silent keepers of a smokeless hearth,
Suddenly cast in the mould of death.

Ancient Ireland, indeed! I was reared by her bedside,
The rune and the chant, evil eye and averted head,
Fomorian fierceness of family and local feud.
Gaunt figures of fear and of friendliness,
For years they trespassed on my dreams,
Until once, in a standing circle of stones,
I felt their shadows pass

Into that dark permanence of ancient forms.

A Lost Tradition

All around, shards of a lost tradition:
From the Rough Field I went to school
In the Glens of the Hazels. Close by
Was the bishopric of the Golden Stone;
The cairn of Carleton's homesick poem.

Scattered over the hills, tribal
And placenames, uncultivated pearls.
No rock or ruin, dun or dolmen
But showed memory defying cruelty
Through an image-encrusted name.

The heathery gap where the Raparee,
Shane Barnagh, saw his brother die—
On a summer's day the dying sun
Stained its colours to crimson:
So breaks the heart, Brish-mo-Cree.

The whole landscape a manuscript
We had lost the skill to read,
A part of our past disinherited;
But fumbled, like a blind man,
Along the fingertips of instinct.

The last Gaelic speaker in the parish
When I stammered my school Irish
One Sunday after mass, crinkled
A rusty litany of praise;
Tá an Ghaedilg againn arís...

Tir Eoghain : Land of Owen,
Province of the O'Niall;
The ghostly tread of O'Hagan's
Barefoot gallowglasses marching
To merge forces in Dun Geanainn

Push southward to Kinsale!
Loudly the war-cry is swallowed
In swirls of black rain and fog
As Ulster's pride, Elizabeth's foemen,
Founder in a Munster bog.

The Siege of Mullingar

At the Fleadh Cheoil in Mullingar
There were two sounds, the breaking
Of glass, and the background pulse
Of music. Young girls roamed
The streets with eager faces,
Pushing for men. Bottles in
Hand, they rowed out for a song:
Puritan Ireland's dead and gone,
A myth of O'Connor and Ó Faoláin.

In the early morning the lovers
Lay on both sides of the canal
Listening on Sony transistors
To the agony of Pope John.
Yet it didn't seem strange or blasphemous,
This ground bass of death and
Resurrection, as we strolled along:
Puritan Ireland's dead and gone,
A myth of O'Connor and Ó Faoláin.

Further on, breasting the wind
Waves of the deserted grain harbour
We saw a pair, a cob and his pen,
Most nobly linked. Everything then
In our casual morning vision
Seemed to flow in one direction,
Line simple as a song:
Puritan Ireland's dead and gone,
A myth of O'Connor and Ó Faoláin.

The Cage

My father, the least happy
man I have known. His face
retained the pallor
of those who work underground:
the lost years in Brooklyn
listening to a subway
shudder the earth.

But a traditional Irishman
who (released from his grille
in the Clark St. I.R.T.)
drank neat whiskey until
he reached the only element
he felt at home in
any longer: brute oblivion.

And yet picked himself
up, most mornings,
to march down the street
extending his smile
to all sides of the good
(non-negro) neighbourhood
belled by St. Teresa's church.

When he came back
we walked together
across fields of Garvaghey
to see hawthorn on the summer
hedges, as though
he had never left;
a bend of the road

which still sheltered
primroses. But we
did not smile in
the shared complicity
of a dream, for when
weary Odysseus returns
Telemachus must leave.

Often as I descend
into subway or underground
I see his bald head behind
the bars of the small booth;
the mark of an old car
accident beating on his
ghostly forehead.

A Drink of Milk

In the girdered dark
of the byre, cattle move;
warm engines hushed
to a siding groove

before the switch flicks
down for milking.
In concrete partitions
they rattle their chains

while the farmhand eases
rubber tentacles to tug
lightly but rhythmically
on their swollen dugs

and up the pale cylinders
of the milking machine
mounts an untouched
steadily pulsing stream.

Only the tabby steals
to dip its radar whiskers
with old fashioned relish
in a chipped saucer

and before Seán lurches
to kick his boots off
in the night-silent kitchen
he draws a mug of froth

to settle on the sideboard
under the hoard of delph.
A pounding transistor shakes
the Virgin on her shelf

as he dreams towards bed.
A last glance at a magazine,
he puts the mug to his head,
grunts, and drains it clean.

Clear the Way

Jimmy Drummond used bad language at school
All the four-letter words, like a drip from a drain.
At six he knew how little children were born
As well he might, since his mother bore nine,
Six after her soldier husband left for the wars

Under the motto of the Inniskillings, *Clear the Way!*
When his body returned from England
The authorities told them not to unscrew the lid
To see the remnants of Fusilier Drummond inside—
a chancy hand-grenade had left nothing to hide

And Jimmy's mother was pregnant at the graveside—
Clear the way, and nothing to hide.
Love came to her punctually each springtime,
Settled in the ditch under some labouring man:
'It comes over you, you have to lie down.'

Her only revenge on her hasty lovers
Was to call each child after its father,
Which the locals admired, and seeing her saunter
To collect the pension of her soldier husband
Trailed by her army of baby Irregulars.

Some of whom made soldiers for foreign wars
Some supplied factories in England.
Jimmy Drummond was the eldest but died younger than
    any
When he fell from a scaffolding in Coventry
Condemned, like all his family, to *Clear the Way!*

A Welcoming Party

Wie war das möglich?

That final newsreel of the war:
A welcoming party of almost shades
Met us at the cinema door
Clicking what remained of their heels.

From nests of bodies like hatching eggs
Flickered insectlike hands and legs
And rose an ululation, terrible, shy;
Children conjugating the verb 'to die'.

One clamoured mutely of love
From a mouth like a burnt glove;
Others upheld hands bleak as begging bowls
Claiming the small change of our souls.

Some smiled at us as protectors.
Can these bones live?
Our parochial brand of innocence
Was all we had to give.

To be always at the periphery of incident
Gave my childhood its Irish dimension; drama of unevent:
Yet doves of mercy, as doves of air,
Can falter here as anywhere.

That long dead Sunday in Armagh
I learned one meaning of total war
And went home to my Christian school
To kick a football through the air.

The Trout

Flat on the bank I parted
Rushes to ease my hands
In the water without a ripple
And tilt them slowly downstream
To where he lay, light as a leaf,
In his fluid sensual dream.

Bodiless lord of creation
I hung briefly above him
Savouring my own absence
Senses expanding in the slow
Motion, the photographic calm
That grows before action.

As the curve of my hands
Swung under his body
He surged, with visible pleasure.
I was so preternaturally close
I could count every stipple
But still cast no shadow, until

The two palms crossed in a cage
Under the lightly pulsing gills.
Then (entering my own enlarged
Shape, which rode on the water)
I gripped. To this day I can
Taste his terror in my hands.

All Legendary Obstacles

All legendary obstacles lay between
Us, the long imaginary plain,
The monstrous ruck of mountains
And, swinging across the night,
Flooding the Sacramento, San Joaquin,
The hissing drift of winter rain.

All day I waited, shifting
Nervously from station to bar
As I saw another train sail
By, the San Francisco Chief or
Golden Gate, water dripping
From great flanged wheels.

At midnight you came, pale
Above the negro porter's lamp.
I was too blind with rain

And doubt to speak, but
Reached from the platform
Until our chilled hands met.

You had been travelling for days
With an old lady, who marked
A neat circle on the glass
With her glove, to watch us
Move into the wet darkness
Kissing, still unable to speak.

Summer Storm

I   *A door banging*

Downstairs, a door
banging, like a
blow upon sleep

pain bleeding
away in gouts
of accusation &

counter accusation:
heart's release
of bitter speech.

II   *Mosquito hunt*

Heat contracts the
walls, smeared with
the bodies of insects

we crush, absurd-
ly balanced on the
springs of the bed

twin shadows on
the wall rising
& falling as

we swoop &
quarrel, like
wide winged bats.

III   *Tides*

The window blown
open, that summer
night, a full moon

occupying the sky
with a pressure of
underwater light

a pale radiance
glossing the titles
behind your head

& the rectangle
of the bed where,
after long separation,

we begin to make
love quietly, bodies
turning like fish

in obedience to
the pull & tug
of your great tides.

The Same Gesture

There is a secret room
of golden light where
everything—love, violence,
hatred is possible;
and, again love.

Such intimacy of hand
and mind is achieved
under its healing light
that the shifting of
hands is a rite

like court music.
We barely know our
selves there though
it is what we always were
—most nakedly are—

and must remember
when we leave, re-
suming our habits
with our clothes:
work, 'phone, drive

through late traffic
changing gears with
the same gesture as
eased your snowbound
heart and flesh.

Herbert Street Revisited

for Madeleine

I

A light is burning late
in this Georgian Dublin street:
someone is leading our old lives!

And our black cat scampers again
through the wet grass of the convent garden
upon his masculine errands.

The pubs shut: a released bull,
Behan shoulders up the street,
topples into our basement, roaring 'John!'

A pony and donkey cropped flank
by flank under the trees opposite;
short neck up, long neck down,

as Nurse Mullen knelt by her bedside
to pray for her lost Mayo hills,
the bruised bodies of Easter Volunteers.

Animals, neighbours, treading the pattern
of one time and place into history,
like our early marriage, while

tall windows looked down upon us
from walls flushed light pink or salmon
watching and enduring succession.

II

As I leave, you whisper,
'don't betray our truth'
and like a ghost dancer,
invoking a lost tribal strength
I halt in tree-fed darkness

to summon back our past,
and celebrate a love that eased
so kindly, the dying bone,
enabling the spirit to sing
of old happiness, when alone.

III

So put the leaves back on the tree,
put the tree back in the ground,
let Brendan trundle his corpse down
the street singing, like Molly Malone.

Let the black cat, tiny emissary
of our happiness, streak again
through the darkness, to fall soft
clawed into a landlord's dustbin.

Let Nurse Mullen take the last
train to Westport, and die upright
in her chair, facing a window
warm with the blue slopes of Nephin.

And let the pony and donkey come—
look, someone has left the gate open—
like hobbyhorses linked in
the slow motion of a dream

parading side by side, down
the length of Herbert Street,
rising and falling, lifting
their hooves through the moonlight.

The Point

Rocks jagged in morning mist.
At intervals, the foghorn sounds
From the white lighthouse rock
Lonely as cow mourning her calf,
Groaning, belly deep, desperate.

I assisted at such failure once;
A night-long fight to save a calf
Born finally, with broken neck.
It flailed briefly on the straw,
A wide-eyed mother straddling it.

Listen carefully. This is different.
It sounds to guide, not lament.
When the defining light is powerless,
Ships hesitating down the strait
Hear its harsh voice as friendliness.

Upstairs my wife and daughter sleep.
Our two lives have separated now
But I would send my voice to yours
Cutting through the shrouding mist
Like some friendly signal in distress.

The fog is lifting, slowly.
Flag high, a new ship is entering.
The opposite shore unveils itself,
Bright in detail as a painting,
Alone, but equal to the morning.

Dowager

I dwell in this leaky Western castle.
American matrons weave across the carpet,
Sorefooted as camels, and less useful.

Smooth Ionic columns hold up a roof.
A chandelier shines on a foxhound's coat:
The grandson of a grandmother I reared.

In the old days I read or embroidered,
But now it is enough to see the sky change,
Clouds extend or smother a mountain's shape.

Wet afternoons I ride in the Rolls;
Windshield wipers flail helpless against the rain:
I thrash through pools like smashing panes of glass.

And the light afterwards! Hedges steam,
I ride through a damp tunnel of sweetness,
The bonnet strewn with bridal hawthorn

From which a silver lady leaps, always young.
Alone, I hum with satisfaction in the sun,
An old bitch, with a warm mouthful of game.

Small Secrets

Where I work
out of doors
children come
to present me
with an acorn
a pine cone—
small secrets—

and a fat
grass snail
who uncoils
to carry his
whorled house
over the top
of my table.

With a pencil
I nudge him
back into
himself, but
fluid horns
unfurl, damp
tentacles, to

probe, test
space before
he drags his
habitation
forward again
on his single
muscular foot

rippling along
its liquid self-
creating path.
With absorbed,
animal faces
the children
watch us both

but he will
have none of
me, the static
angular world
of books, papers—
which is neither
green nor moist—

only to climb
around, over
as with rest-
less glistening
energy, he races
at full tilt
over the ledge

onto the grass.
All I am left
with is, between
pine cone & acorn
the silver smear
of his progress
which will soon

wear off, like
the silvery galaxies,
mother of pearl
motorways, woven
across the grass
each morning by
the tireless snails

of the world,
minute as grains
of rice, gross
as conch or
triton, bequeath-
ing their shells
to the earth.

JAMES SIMMONS b. 1933

The Influence of Natural Objects
for Bill Ireland

Night after night from our camp on Sugar Loaf Hill
We strolled the streets, roaring or quiet, daring
Anything for girls or drink, but not caring
When the town closed. We reeled home and were ill,
Cooked fries, fell senseless in our socks
On grass or blankets. I woke cold at dawn
And stumbled to the Hill Top Zoo, and on
Through pines to the bare summit's litter of rocks.
I was always scared by the huge spaces below,
Between sky and water, explosive bright air
Glinting on live-wire nerves of mine, worn bare.
I lay down, grinning, stiff with vertigo.

This roused an appetite for breakfast, bars,
Bathing, chasing the daft holiday bitches,
For jokes and poems, beer and sandwiches...
And so on till we slept under the stars.

Outward Bound
for Tony Harrison

Two campers (King Lear and his clown?)
Smile to see the skies come down.
The shaken mind finds metaphors
In winds that shake the great outdoors.
As roofs and fences fall in storms
The tranquil mind's protective forms
Collapse when passion, grief and fear
Stir. We will spend a fortnight here.

To this small wilderness we bring
Ourselves to play at suffering,
To swim in lonely bays, immerse

In the destructive elements, nurse
Our bare forked bodies by wood fires
Where ox-tail soup in mugs inspires
The tender flesh. By rocks we cough
And shiver in the wind, throw off
What history has lent and lie
Naked, alone, under the sky.

Of course, not one of us prefers
The cold; we are sun-worshippers,
Wilderness- and storm-defiers,
Neither masochists nor liars.

Cheeks whipped by freezing rain go numb.
The baffled blood is stirred, will come
Again, glowing like my mind when Lear
Speaks in the words of Shakespeare.
Under duress trying to sing
In tune, foretasting suffering
That we will swallow whole, the storm
Endured, we hope to come to harm
At home, with better dignity
Or style or courage. Anyway
I like to camp and read *King Lear*.
We had a lovely fortnight here.

Stephano Remembers

We broke out of our dream into a clearing
and there were all our masters still sneering.
My head bowed, I made jokes and turned away,
living over and over that strange day.

The ship struck before morning. Half past four,
on a huge hogshead of claret I swept ashore
like an evangelist aboard his god:
his will was mine, I laughed and kissed the rod,
and would have walked that foreign countryside
blind drunk, contentedly till my god died;
but finding Trinculo made it a holiday:
two Neapolitans had got away,
and that shipload of scheming toffs we hated
was drowned. Never to be humiliated
again, 'I will no more to sea,' I sang.
Down white empty beaches my voice rang,
and that dear monster, half fish and half man,
went on his knees to me. Oh, Caliban,
you thought I'd take your twisted master's life;
but a drunk butler's slower with a knife
than your fine courtiers, your dukes, your kings.
We were distracted by too many things...
the wine, the jokes, the music, fancy gowns.
We were no good as murderers, we were clowns.

Lullaby for Rachael

All your days are holy days,
in dreams begins your terror.
Predetermined are the ways
perfection comes to error.

Flaws, like hands used in the sun,
will gradually harden.
You, as your elders did, will run
from simple things, from the garden.

Sleeping when each day is through
practise for your death.
Learn each law you're subject to
within your lease of breath.

My world is mapped imperfectly:
here I once found treasure,
friends here, here the enemy;
alter it with pleasure.

Changing the boundary lines, I fear,
has made my map a mess.
By seeing more you may draw clear,
but not by seeing less.

The lullaby was adequate,
you'll sleep until the morning.
How little we communicate,
how useless is this warning.

Though I have failed to make you wise
with all the words above,
I've made, while trying to tell no lies,
a noise to go with love.

Goodbye, Sally

Shaken already, I know
I'll wake at night after you go
watching the soft shine of your skin,
feeling your little buttocks, oh my grief,
like two duck eggs in a handkerchief,
barely a woman but taking me all in.

I think our love won't die—
but there I go trying to justify!
What odds that we'll never meet again
and probably other girls will never
bring half your agony of pleasure?
Fidelity is a dumb pain.

God, but I'm lucky too,
the way I've muddled through
to ecstasy so often despite
exhaustion, drunkenness and pride.
How come that you were satisfied
and so was I that night?

It's true for drinker and lover,
the best stuff has no hangover.
You're right to spit on argument,
girl. Your dumbness on a walk
was better than my clown's talk.
You showed me what you meant.

Good mornings from every night
with you, thirsty and sore with appetite.
You never let me act my age.
Goodbye to all analysis and cause-
grubbing. The singer wants applause
not criticism as he leaves the stage.

Join Me in Celebrating

Join me in celebrating
This unhoped for gift
She has brought me sweating
In a crumpled shift.
Pushed through my wife,
My letter-box, appears
A present of life,
Bald head and flattened ears,
Parcelled in blood and slime,
A loosely wrapped thing
Unlabelled but on time,
String dangling.
I wouldn't change my condition
For freedom, cash, applause,
Rebirth of young ambition
Or faith in Santa Claus.

A Birthday Poem
for Rachael

For every year of life we light
a candle on your cake
to mark the simple sort of progress
anyone can make,
and then, to test your nerve or give
a proper view of death,
you're asked to blow each light, each year,
out with your own breath.

Letter to a Jealous Friend

You could not say, 'What now?' you said, 'Too late!'
What energies bad principles have spilt.
Old friend, you hate me and you aggravate
Me, for I will not feel regret or guilt

When your white face stares at me from the door
With wizard eyes that change the three of us
Into a cuckold, a roué, a whore—
A stupid, ugly metamorphosis.

Acquaintances are mocking my belief
That we could still be friends when it was known.
I tremble when you treat me like a thief;
But I touched nothing you can call your own.

A child might own the doll it sleeps beside
And men own money and what money buys;
But no one earns a friend or owns his bride
However much he needs or hard he tries.

You try to run me over with your bus
And call me out of restaurants to fight.
I smile weakly and wait for all the fuss
To fade. I need to get my sleep at night.

I hear in some domestic tiff she tossed
Our love at you and scored. Each time I try
To fit that in my creed I lose my place.
There's more in animals than meets the eye.

Sweet fun and freedom didn't last for long
With you out shouting we'd betrayed your trust.
We said it was our business. We were wrong.
Your jealousy's as natural as our lust.

Our thoughts of other people paralyse
Our minds and make us act the silly parts
We think they cast us in. Feeling their eyes
On us, we seem to lose touch with our hearts.

Crippled by hate you have to crouch in dude
Levis and dark glasses, glaring at us.
We have to lie unnaturally nude
And vulnerable, trapped, ridiculous.

Art and Reality
for James Boyce

From twenty yards I saw my old love
locking up her car.
She smiled and waved, as lovely still
As girls of twenty are—

That cloud of auburn hair that bursts
Like sunrise round her head,
The smile that made me smile
At ordinary things she said.

But twenty years have gone and flesh
Is perishable stuff;
Can art and exercise and diet
Ever be enough

To save the tiny facial muscles
And keep taut the skin
And have the waist, in middle-age,
Still curving firmly in?

Beauty invites me to approach
And lies make truth seem hard
As my old love assumes her age,
A year for every yard.

One of the Boys

Our youth was gay but rough,
much drink and copulation.
If that seems not enough
blame our miseducation.
In shabby boarding houses
lips covered lips,
and in our wild carouses
there were companionships.
Cheap and mundane the setting
of all that we remember:
in August, dance-hall petting,
cinemas in December.
Now middle-aged I know,
and do not hide the truth,
used or misused years go
and take all kinds of youth.
We test the foreign scene
or grow too fat in banks,
salesmen for margarine,
soldiers in tanks,
the great careers all tricks,
the fine arts all my arse,
business and politics
a cruel farce.
Though fear of getting fired
may ease, and work is hated
less, we are tired, tired
and incapacitated.
On golf courses, in bars,
crutched by the cash we earn,
we think of nights in cars
with energy to burn.

In Memoriam: Judy Garland

At forty-seven Frances Gumm is dead,
A plump, unhappy child who got ahead.

Towards the moon from her ecstatic face
Notes soared. The moon is an awful place.

She sang of a land heard of, held by her gross
Society, administering drugs, an overdose.

Discs are turning. Needles touch the rings
Of dark rainbows. Judy Garland sings.

Didn't He Ramble

for Michael Longley

'The family wanted to make a bricklayer of him, but Ferd. was too smooth and clever a fellow. He preferred to sit in the parlour out of the sun and play piano.'

Henry Morton

There was a hardware shop in Main Street sold
records as well as spades and plastic bowls.
Jo, the assistant, had a taste for jazz.
The shop being empty as it mostly was
I tried out records, then, like seeing the light,
but genuine, I heard Josh White:
I'M GOING TO MO-O-VE YOU, WAY ON THE OUTSKIRTS
    OF TOWN.
Where was my turntable to set it down!
A voice styled by experience, learning to make
music listening to Blind Willie Blake,
walking the streets of a city, avoiding cops,
toting a cheap guitar and begging box.

The campus poets used to write of saxophones
disgustedly and sneer at gramophones;
but the word of life, if such a thing existed,
was there on record among the rubbish listed
in the catalogues of Brunswick and H.M.V.,
healing the split in sensibility.
Tough reasonableness and lyric grace
together, in poor man's dialect.
Something that no one taught us to expect.
Profundity without the po-face
of court and bourgeois modes. This I could use
to live and die with. Jazz. Blues.
I love the music and the men who made
the music, and instruments they played:
saxophone, piano, trumpet, clarinet,
Bill Broonzy, Armstrong, Basie, Hodges, Chet
Baker, Garner, Tommy Ladnier,
Jelly Roll Morton, Bessie Smith, Bechet,
and Fats Waller, the scholar-clown of song
who sang, *Until the Real Thing Comes Along*.
Here was the risen people, their feet
dancing, not out to murder the elite:
'Pardon me, sir, may we be free?
The kitchen staff is having a jamboree.'

History records how people cleared the shelves
of record shops, discovering themselves,
making distinctions in the ordinary,
seeing what they'd been too tired to see;
but most ignored the music. Some were scared,
some greedy, some condemned what they hadn't heard,
some sold cheap imitations, watered it down,
bribed Fats to drink too much and play the clown
instead of the piano, and failed—the man was wise,
he did both painlessly. Jazz is a compromise:
you take the first tune in your head and play
until it's saying what you want to say.
'I ain't got no diplomas,' said Satchmo,
'I look into my heart and blow.'

What if some great ones took to drugs and drink
and killed themselves? Only a boy could think
the world cures easy, and want to blame
someone. I know I'll never be the same
A mad world my masters! We might have known
that Wardell Gray was only well spoken,
controlled and elegant on saxophone.
He appeared last in a field with his neck broken.
The jazz life did it, not the Ku Klux Klan.
Whatever made the music killed the man.

SEAMUS HEANEY b. 1939

Follower

My father worked with a horse-plough,
His shoulders globed like a full sail strung
Between the shafts and the furrow.
The horses strained at his clicking tongue.

An expert. He would set the wing
And fit the bright steel-pointed sock.
The sod rolled over without breaking.
At the headrig, with a single pluck

Of reins, the sweating team turned round
And back into the land. His eye
Narrowed and angled at the ground,
Mapping the furrow exactly.

I stumbled in his hob-nailed wake,
Fell sometimes on the polished sod;
Sometimes he rode me on his back
Dipping and rising to his plod.

I wanted to grow up and plough,
To close one eye, stiffen my arm.
All I ever did was follow
In his broad shadow round the farm.

I was a nuisance, tripping, falling,
Yapping always. But today
It is my father who keeps stumbling
Behind me, and will not go away.

Mossbawn: Two Poems in Dedication

for Mary Heaney

1.   Sunlight

There was a sunlit absence.
The helmeted pump in the yard
heated its iron,
water honeyed

in the slung bucket
and the sun stood
like a griddle cooling
against the wall

of each long afternoon.
So, her hands scuffled
over the bakeboard,
the reddening stove

sent its plaque of heat
against her where she stood
in a floury apron
by the window.

Now she dusts the board
with a goose's wing,
now sits, broad-lapped,
with whitened nails

and measling shins:
here is a space
again, the scone rising
to the tick of two clocks.

And here is love
like a tinsmith's scoop
sunk past its gleam
in the meal-bin.

2.   The seed cutters

They seem hundreds of years away. Breughel,
You'll know them if I can get them true.
They kneel under the hedge in a half-circle
Behind a windbreak wind is breaking through.
They are the seed cutters. The tuck and frill
Of leaf-sprout is on the seed potatoes
Buried under that straw. With time to kill
They are taking their time. Each sharp knife goes
Lazily halving each root that falls apart
In the palm of the hand: a milky gleam,
And, at the centre, a dark watermark.
O calendar customs! Under the broom
Yellowing over them, compose the frieze
With all of us there, our anonymities.

The Peninsula

When you have nothing more to say, just drive
For a day all round the peninsula.
The sky is tall as over a runway,
The land without marks so you will not arrive

But pass through, though always skirting landfall.
At dusk, horizons drink down sea and hill,
The ploughed field swallows the whitewashed gable
And you're in the dark again. Now recall

The glazed foreshore and silhouetted log,
That rock where breakers shredded into rags,
The leggy birds stilted on their own legs,
Islands riding themselves out into the fog

And drive back home, still with nothing to say
Except that now you will uncode all landscapes
By this: things founded clean on their own shapes,
Water and ground in their extremity.

Bogland
for T. P. Flanagan

We have no prairies
To slice a big sun at evening—
Everywhere the eye concedes to
Encroaching horizon,

Is wooed into the cyclops' eye
Of a tarn. Our unfenced country
Is bog that keeps crusting
Between the sights of the sun.

They've taken the skeleton
Of the Great Irish Elk
Out of the peat, set it up
An astounding crate full of air.

Butter sunk under
More than a hundred years
Was recovered salty and white.
The ground itself is kind, black butter

Melting and opening underfoot,
Missing its last definition
By millions of years.
They'll never dig coal here,

Only the waterlogged trunks
Of great firs, soft as pulp.
Our pioneers keep striking
Inwards and downwards,

Every layer they strip
Seems camped on before.
The bogholes might be Atlantic seepage.
The wet centre is bottomless.

The Tollund Man

1

Some day I will go to Aarhus
To see his peat-brown head,
The mild pods of his eye-lids,
His pointed skin cap.

In the flat country nearby
Where they dug him out,
His last gruel of winter seeds
Caked in his stomach,

Naked except for
The cap, noose and girdle,
I will stand a long time.
Bridegroom to the goddess,

She tightened her torc on him
And opened her fen,
Those dark juices working
Him to a saint's kept body,

Trove of the turfcutters'
Honeycombed workings.
Now his stained face
Reposes at Aarhus.

2

I could risk blasphemy,
Consecrate the cauldron bog
Our holy ground and pray
Him to make germinate

The scattered, ambushed
Flesh of labourers,
Stockinged corpses
Laid out in the farmyards,

Tell-tale skin and teeth
Flecking the sleepers
Of four young brothers, trailed
For miles along the lines.

3

Something of his sad freedom
As he rode the tumbril
Should come to me, driving,
Saying the names

Tollund, Grabaulle, Nebelgard,
Watching the pointing hands
Of country people,
Not knowing their tongue.

Out there in Jutland
In the old man-killing parishes
I will feel lost,
Unhappy and at home.

Strange Fruit

Here is the girl's head like an exhumed gourd.
Oval-faced, prune-skinned, prune-stones for teeth.
They unswaddled the wet fern of her hair
And made an exhibition of its coil,
Let the air at her leathery beauty.
Pash of tallow, perishable treasure:
Her broken nose is dark as a turf clod,
Her eyeholes blank as pools in the old workings.
Diodorus Siculus confessed
His gradual ease among the likes of this:
Murdered, forgotten, nameless, terrible
Beheaded girl, outstaring axe
And beatification, outstaring
What had begun to feel like reverence.

Undine

He slashed the briars, shovelled up grey silt
To give me right of way in my own drains
And I ran quick for him, cleaned out my rust.

He halted, saw me finally disrobed,
Running clear, with apparent unconcern.
Then he walked by me. I rippled and I churned

Where ditches intersected near the river
Until he dug a spade deep in my flank
And took me to him. I swallowed his trench

Gratefully, dispersing myself for love
Down in his roots, climbing his brassy grain—
But once he knew my welcome, I alone

Could give him subtle increase and reflection.
He explored me so completely, each limb
Lost its cold freedom. Human, warmed to him.

The Wife's Tale

When I had spread it all on linen cloth
Under the hedge, I called them over.
The hum and gulp of the thresher ran down
And the big belt slewed to a standstill, straw
Hanging undelivered in the jaws.
There was such quiet that I heard their boots
Crunching the stubble twenty yards away.

He lay down and said 'Give these fellows theirs.
I'm in no hurry,' plucking grass in handfuls
And tossing it in the air. 'That looks well.'
(He nodded at my white cloth on the grass.)
'I declare a woman could lay out a field
Though boys like us have little call for cloths.'
He winked, then watched me as I poured a cup
And buttered the thick slices that he likes.
'It's threshing better than I thought, and mind
It's good clean seed. Away over there and look.'
Always this inspection has to be made
Even when I don't know what to look for.

But I ran my hand in the half-filled bags
Hooked to the slots. It was hard as shot,
Innumerable and cool. The bags gaped
Where the chutes ran back to the stilled drum
And forks were stuck at angles in the ground
As javelins might mark lost battlefields.
I moved between them back across the stubble.

They lay in the ring of their own crusts and dregs
Smoking and saying nothing. 'There's good yield,
Isn't there?'—as proud as if he were the land itself—
'Enough for crushing and for sowing both.'
And that was it. I'd come and he had shown me
So I belonged no further to the work.
I gathered cups and folded up the cloth
And went. But they still kept their ease
Spread out, unbuttoned, grateful, under the trees.

Wedding Day

I am afraid.
Sound has stopped in the day
And the images reel over
And over. Why all those tears,

The wild grief on his face
Outside the taxi? The sap
Of mourning rises
In our waving guests.

You sing behind the tall cake
Like a deserted bride
Who persists, demented,
And goes through the ritual.

When I went to the gents
There was a skewered heart
And a legend of love. Let me
Sleep in your breast to the airport.

from Whatever You Say, Say Nothing

This morning from a dewy motorway
I saw the new camp for the internees:
A bomb had left a crater of fresh clay
In the roadside, and over in the trees

Machine-gun posts defined a real stockade.
There was that white mist you get on a low ground
And it was déjà-vu, some film made
Of Stalag 17, a bad dream with no sound.

Is there a life before death? That's chalked up
In Ballymurphy. Competence with pain,
Coherent miseries, a bite and sup,
We hug our little destiny again.

Exposure

It is December in Wicklow:
Alders dripping, birches
Inheriting the last light,
The ash tree cold to look at.

A comet that was lost
Should be visible at sunset,
Those million tons of light
Like a glimmer of haws and rose-hips,

And I sometimes see a falling star.
If I could come on meteorite!
Instead I walk through damp leaves,
Husks, the spent flukes of autumn,

Imagining a hero
On some muddy compound,
His gift like a slingstone
Whirled for the desperate.

How did I end up like this?
I often think of my friends'
Beautiful prismatic counselling
And the anvil brains of some who hate me

As I sit weighing and weighing
My responsible *tristia*.
For what? For the ear? For the people?
For what is said behind-backs?

Rain comes down through the alders,
Its low conducive voices
Mutter about let-downs and erosions
And yet each drop recalls

The diamond absolutes.
I am neither internee nor informer;
An inner émigré, grown long-haired
And thoughtful; a wood-kerne

Escaped from the massacre,
Taking protective colouring
From bole and bark, feeling
Every wind that blows;

Who, blowing up these sparks
For their meagre heat, have missed
The once-in-a-lifetime portent,
The comet's pulsing rose.

MICHAEL LONGLEY b. 1939

Graffiti

It would be painful, tedious and late
To alter awkward monsters such as these
To charming princes—metamorphoses
That all good fairy tales accelerate—

One kiss and, in the twinkling of an eye,
The Calibans accepted, warts and all,
At long last resurrected from the sty,
So blond, so beautiful, and six feet tall.

Through billboard forests, mists of lingerie,
These track a princess unequipped to change
Herself or them: her hair no winds derange,
Her thighs are locked, her cleavage legendary.

Lips where large allure but no response is,
Her all too perfect body they endure
By pencilling these bouquets of moustaches
As love's own emblem, their own signature.

Despite an aura vast enough to toss
Her neon constellations through the land,
She, in a realm too fragile to withstand
A single hair that is superfluous,

In paper palaces lies wintering,
While these who decorate her lovely crotch
With pubic shrubbery and with a notch,
Unwittingly imply a sort of spring—

Such passion thwarted, such artistry released!
O where would Beauty be without her Beast?

Circe

The cries of the shipwrecked enter my head.
On wildest nights when the torn sky confides
Its face to the sea's cracked mirror, my bed
—Addressed by the moon and her tutored tides—

Through brainstorm, through nightmare and ocean
Keeps me afloat. Shallows are my coven,
The comfortable margins—in this notion
I stand uncorrected by the sun even.

Out of the night husband after husband
—Eyes wide as oysters, arms full of driftwood—
Wades ashore and puts in at my island.
My necklaces of sea shells and sea weed,

My skirts of spindrift, sandals of flotsam
Catch the eye of each bridegroom for ever.
Quite forgetful of the widowing calm
My sailors wait through bad and good weather.

At first in rock pools I become their wife,
Under the dunes at last they lie with me—
These are the spring and neap tides of their life.
I have helped so many sailors off the sea,

And, counting no man among my losses,
I have made of my arms and my thighs last rooms
For the irretrievable and capsized—
I extend the sea, its idioms.

Epithalamion

These are the small hours when
Moths by their fatal appetite
That brings them tapping to get in,
    Are steered along the night
To where our window catches light.

Who hazard all to be
Where we, the only two it seems,
Inhabit so delightfully
    A room it bursts its seams
And spills on to the lawn in beams,

Such visitors as these
Reflect with eyes like frantic stars
This garden's brightest properties,
    Cruising its corridors
Of light above the folded flowers,

Till our vicinity
Is rendered royal by their flight
Towards us, till more silently
    The silent stars ignite,
Their aeons dwindling by a night,

And everything seems bent
On robing in this evening you
And me, all dark the element
    Our light is earnest to,
All quiet gathered round us who,

When over the embankments
A train that's loudly reprobate
Shoots from silence into silence,
    With ease accommodate
Its pandemonium, its freight.

I hold you close because
We have decided dark will be
For ever like this and because,
    My love, already
The dark is growing elderly.

With dawn upon its way,
Punctually and as a rule,
The small hours widening into day,
Our room its vestibule
Before it fills all houses full,

We too must hazard all,
Switch off the lamp without a word
For the last of night assembled
Over it and unperturbed
By the moth that lies there littered,

And notice how the trees
Which took on anonymity
Are again in their huge histories
Displayed, that wherever we
Attempt, and as far as we can see,

The flowers everywhere
Are withering, the stars dissolved,
Amalgamated in a glare,
Which last night were revolved
Discreetly round us—and, involved,

The two of us, in these
Which early morning has deformed,
Must hope that in new properties
We'll find a uniform
To know each other truly by, or,

At the least, that these will,
When we rise, be seen with dawn
As remnant yet part raiment still,
Like flags that linger on
The sky when king and queen are gone.

No Continuing City

My hands here, gentle, where her breasts begin,
My picture in her eyes—
It is time for me to recognise
This new dimension, my last girl.
So, to set my house in order, I imagine
Photographs, advertisements—the old lies,
The lumber of my soul—

All that is due for spring cleaning,
Everything that soul-destroys.
Into the open I bring
Girls who linger still in photostat
(For whom I was so many different boys)—
I explode their myths before it is too late,
Their promises I detonate—

There is quite a lot that I can do...
I leave them—are they six or seven, two or three?—
Locked in their small geographies.
The hillocks of their bodies' lovely shires
(Whose all weathers I have walked through)
Acre by acre recede entire
To summer country.

From collision to eclipse their case is closed.
Who took me by surprise
Like comets first—now, failing to ignite,
They constellate such uneventful skies,
Their stars arranged each night
In the old stories
Which I successfully have diagnosed.

Though they momentarily survive
In my delays,
They neither cancel nor improve
My continuing city with old ways,
Familiar avenues to love—
Down my one way streets (it is time to finish)
Their eager syllables diminish.

Though they call out from the suburbs
Of experience—they know how that disturbs!—
Or, already tending towards home,
Prepare to hitch-hike on the kerbs,
Their bags full of dear untruths—
I am their medium
And I take the words out of their mouths.

From today new hoardings crowd my eyes,
Pasted over my ancient histories
Which (I must be cruel to be kind)
Only gale or cloudburst now discover,
Ripping the billboard of my mind—
Oh, there my lovers,
There my dead no longer advertise.

I transmit from the heart a closing broadcast
To my girl, my bride, my wife-to-be—
I tell her she is welcome,
Advising her to make this last,
To be sure of finding room in me
(I embody bed and breakfast)—
To eat and drink me out of house and home.

Swans Mating

Even now I wish that you had been there
Sitting beside me on the riverbank:
The cob and his pen sailing in rhythm
Until their small heads met and the final
Heraldic moment dissolved in ripples.

This was a marriage and a baptism,
A holding of breath, nearly a drowning,
Wings spread wide for balance where he trod,
Her feathers full of water and her neck
Under the water like a bar of light.

The Goose

Remember the white goose in my arms,
A present still. I plucked the long
Flight-feathers, down from the breast,
Finest fuzz from underneath the wings.

I thought of you through the operation
And covered the unmolested head,
The pink eyes that had persisted in
An expression of disappointment.

It was right to hesitate before
I punctured the skin, made incisions
And broached with my reluctant fingers
The chill of its intestines, because

Surviving there, lodged in its tract,
Nudging the bruise of the orifice
Was the last egg. I delivered it
Like clean bone, a seamless cranium.

Much else followed which, for your sake,
I bundled away, burned on the fire
With the head, the feet, the perfect wings.
The goose was ready for the oven.

I would boil the egg for your breakfast,
Conserve for weeks the delicate fats
As in the old days. In the meantime
We dismantled it, limb by limb.

Caravan

A rickety chimney suggests
The diminutive stove,
Children perhaps, the pots
And pans adding up to love—

So much concentrated under
The low roof, the windows
Shuttered against snow and wind,
That you would be magnified

(If you were there) by the dark,
Wearing it like an apron
And revolving in your hands
As weather in a glass dome,

The blizzard, the day beyond
And—tiny, barely in focus—
Me disappearing out of view
On probably the only horse,

Cantering off to the right
To collect the week's groceries,
Or to be gone for good
Having drawn across my eyes

Like a curtain all that light
And the snow, my history
Stiffening with the tea towels
Hung outside the door to dry.

The Adulterer

I have laid my adulteries
Beneath the floorboards, then resettled
The linoleum so that
The pattern aligns exactly,

Or, when I bundled into the cupboard
Their loose limbs, their heads,
I papered over the door
And cut a hole for the handle.

There they sleep with their names,
My other women, their underwear
Disarranged a little,
Their wounds closing slowly.

I have watched in the same cracked cup
Each separate face dissolve,
Their dispositions
Cluster like tea leaves,

Folding a silence about my hands
Which infects the mangle,
The hearth rug, the kitchen chair
I've been meaning to get mended.

Company

I imagine a day when the children
Are drawers full of soft toys, photographs
Beside the only surviving copies
Of the books that summarise my lifetime,
And I have begun to look forward to
Retirement, second childhood, except that
Love has diminished to one high room

Below which the vigilantes patrol
While I attempt to make myself heard
Above the cacophonous plumbing, and you
Who are my solitary interpreter
Can bear my company for long enough
To lipread such fictions as I believe
Will placate remote customs officials,
The border guards, or even reassure
Anxious butchers, greengrocers, tradesmen
On whom we depend for our daily bread,
The dissemination of manuscripts,
News from the outside world, simple acts
Of such unpatriotic generosity
That until death we hesitate together
On the verge of an almost total silence:

Or else we are living in the country
In a far-off townland divided by
The distances it takes to overhear
A quarrel or the sounds of love-making,
Where even impoverished households
Can afford to focus binoculars
On our tiny windows, the curtains
That wear my motionless silhouette
As I sit late beside a tilley-lamp
And try to put their district on the map
And to name the fields for them, for you
Who busy yourself about the cottage,
Its thatch letting in, the tall grasses
And the rain leaning against the half-door,
Dust on the rafters and our collection
Of curious utensils, pots and pans
The only escape from which is the twice
Daily embarrassed journey to and from
The well we have choked with alder branches
For the cattle's safety, their hoofprints
A thirsty circle in the puddles,
Watermarks under all that we say.

In Memoriam

My father, let no similes eclipse
Where crosses like some forest simplified
Sink roots into my mind, the slow sands
Of your history delay till through your eyes
I read you like a book. Before you died,
Re-enlisting with all the broken soldiers
You bent beneath your rucksack, near collapse,
In anecdote rehearsed and summarised
These words I write in memory. Let yours
And other heartbreaks play into my hands.

Now I see in close-up, in my mind's eye,
The cracked and splintered dead for pity's sake
Each dismal evening predecease the sun,
You, looking death and nightmare in the face
With your kilt, harmonica and gun,
Grow older in a flash, but none the wiser
(Who, following the wrong queue at The Palace,
Have joined the London Scottish by mistake),
Your nineteen years uncertain if and why
Belgium put the kibosh on the Kaiser.

Between the corpses and the soup canteens
You swooned away, watching your future spill.
But, as it was, your proper funeral urn
Had mercifully smashed to smithereens,
To shrapnel shards that sliced your testicle.
That instant I, your most unlikely son,
In No Man's Land was surely left for dead,
Blotted out from your far horizon.
As your voice now is locked inside my head,
I yet was held secure, waiting my turn.

Finally, that lousy war was over.
Stranded in France and in need of proof
You hunted down experimental lovers,
Persuading chorus girls and countesses:
This, father, the last confidence you spoke.

In my twentieth year your old wounds woke
As cancer. Lodging under the same roof
Death was a visitor who hung about,
Strewing the house with pills and bandages,
Till he chose to put your spirit out.

Though they overslept the sequence of events
Which ended with the ambulance outside,
You lingering in the hall, your bowels on fire,
Tears in your eyes, and all your medals spent,
I summon girls who packed at last and went
Underground with you. Their souls again on hire,
Now those lost wives as recreated brides
Take shape before me, materialise.
On the verge of light and happy legend
They lift their skirts like blinds across your eyes.

Wounds

Here are two pictures from my father's head—
I have kept them like secrets until now:
First, the Ulster Division at the Somme
Going over the top with 'Fuck the Pope!'
'No Surrender!': a boy about to die,
Screaming 'Give 'em one for the Shankill!'
'Wilder than Gurkhas' were my father's words
Of admiration and bewilderment.
Next comes the London-Scottish padre
Resettling kilts with his swagger-stick,
With a stylish backhand and a prayer.
Over a landscape of dead buttocks
My father followed him for fifty years.

At last, a belated casualty,
He said—lead traces flaring till they hurt—
'I am dying for King and Country, slowly.'
I touched his hand, his thin head I touched.

Now, with military honours of a kind,
With his badges, his medals like rainbows,
His spinning compass, I bury beside him
Three teenage soldiers, bellies full of
Bullets and Irish beer, their flies undone.
A packet of Woodbines I throw in,
A lucifer, the Sacred Heart of Jesus
Paralysed as heavy guns put out
The night-light in a nursery for ever;
Also a bus-conductor's uniform—
He collapsed beside his carpet-slippers
Without a murmur, shot through the head
By a shivering boy who wandered in
Before they could turn the television down
Or tidy away the supper dishes.
To the children, to a bewildered wife,
I think 'Sorry Missus' was what he said.

Fleance

I entered with a torch before me
And cast my shadow on the backcloth
Momentarily: a handful of words,
One bullet with my initials on it—
And that got stuck in a property tree.

I would have caught it between my teeth
Or, a true professional, stood still
While the two poetic murderers
Pinned my silhouette to history
In a shower of accurate daggers.

But as any illusionist might
Unfasten the big sack of darkness,
The ropes and handcuffs, and emerge
Smoking a nonchalant cigarette,
I escaped—only to lose myself.

It took me a lifetime to explore
The dusty warren beneath the stage
With its trapdoor opening on to
All that had happened above my head
Like noises-off or distant weather.

In the empty auditorium I bowed
To one preoccupied caretaker
And, without removing my make-up,
Hurried back to the digs where Banquo
Sat up late with a hole in his head.

SEAMUS DEANE b. 1940

Return

The train shot through the dark.
Hedges leapt across the window-pane.
Trees belled in foliage were stranded,
Inarticulate with rain.
A blur of lighted farm implied
The evacuated countryside.

I am appalled by its emptiness.
Every valley glows with pain
As we run like a current through;
Then the memories darken again.
In this Irish past I dwell
Like sound implicit in a bell.

The train curves round a river,
And how tenderly its gouts of steam
Contemplate the nodding moon
The waters from the clouds redeem.
Two hours from Belfast
I am snared in my past.

Crusts of light lie pulsing
Diamanté with the rain
At the track's end. Amazing!
I am in Derry once again.
Once more I turn to greet
Ground that flees from my feet.

Roots

Younger,
I felt the dead
Drag at my feet
Like roots
And at every step
I heard them
Crying
Stop.

Older,
I heard the roots
Snap. The crying
Stopped. Ever since
I have been
Dying
Slowly
From the top.

A Schooling

Ice in the school-room, listen,
The high authority of the cold
On some November morning
Turning to fragile crystals
In the Government milk
I was drinking and my world
All frost and snow, chalk and ice;
Quadratic equations on the board
Shining and shifting in white
Isosceles steps. In that trance
What could I know of his labour?
I, in my infinitesimally perceptive dance,
Thought nothing of the harbour
Where, in his fifth hour,

150

Waist-deep in water,
He laid cables, rode the dour
Iron swell between his legs
And maybe thought what kind of son,
An aesthetician of this cold,
He had, in other warmth, begot?
But there's ice in the school-room,
Father. Listen. The harbour's empty.
The Government's milk has been drunk.
It lies on the stomach yet, freezing,
Its kindness, inhuman, has sunk
In where up starts the feeling
That pitches a cold in the thought
Of authority's broken milk crystals
On the lips of the son you begot.

Fording the River

Sunday afternoon and the water
Black among the stones, the forest
Ash-grey in its permanent dusk
Of unquivering pine. That day
You unexpectedly crossed the river.

It was cold and you quickly shouted
As your feet felt the wet white stones
Knocking together. I had bent
To examine a strand of barbed wire
Looping up from a buried fence

When I heard you shout. And,
There you were, on the other side,
Running away. In a slow puncturing

Of anticipation I shivered
As if you had, unpermitted, gone for ever,

Gone, although you were already in the middle
Coming back; I picked up
Your shoes with a sense that years
Had suddenly decided to pass.
I remembered your riddle

On the way up here. ' "Brother or sister
I have none, but that man's father
Is my father's son." Who am I
Talking about?' About my son,
Who crossed cold Lethe, thought it Rubicon.

The Brethren

Arraigned by silence, I recall
The noise of lecture-rooms,
School refectories and dining hall,
A hundred faces in a hundred spoons,
Raised in laughter or in prayer bent,
Each distorted and each innocent.

Torrential sunlight falling through the slats
Made marquetries of light upon the floor.
I still recall those greasy Belfast flats
Where parties hit upon a steady roar
Of subdued violence and lent
Fury to the Sabbath which we spent

Hung over empty streets where Jimmy Witherspoon
Sang under the needle old laments
Of careless love and the indifferent moon,
Evoked the cloudy drumbrush scents
Of Negro brothels while our Plymouth Brethren,
Two doors down, sat sunk in heaven.

Stupor Sunday, *stupor mundi*. What was to come?
The plaints that were growing
Their teeth in the jaws of their aquarium
Sunday's splashless, deep-sown
Peace? What if it were shattered?
Our noise was life and life mattered.

Recently I found old photographs
Fallen behind the attic water-tank
And saw my friends were now the staffs
Of great bureaucracies. Some frames stank
Of mildew, some were so defaced
That half the time I couldn't put a face

On half of them. Some were dead.
The water had seeped through a broken housing,
Had slowly savaged all those eyes and heads.
I felt its rusted coldness dousing
Those black American blues-fired tunes,
The faces echoed in those hammered spoons.

DEREK MAHON b. 1941

In Carrowdore Churchyard

at the grave of Louis MacNeice

Your ashes will not stir, even on this high ground,
However the wind tugs, the headstones shake—
This plot is consecrated, for your sake,
To what lies in the future tense. You lie
Past tension now, and spring is coming round
Igniting flowers on the peninsula.

Your ashes will not fly, however the rough winds burst
Through the wild brambles and the reticent trees.
All we may ask of you we have. The rest
Is not for publication, will not be heard.
Maguire, I believe, suggested a blackbird
And over your grave a phrase from Euripides.

Which suits you down to the ground, like this churchyard
With its play of shadow, its humane perspective.
Locked in the winter's fist, these hills are hard
As nails, yet soft and feminine in their turn
When fingers open and the hedges burn.
This, you implied, is how we ought to live—

The ironical, loving crush of roses against snow,
Each fragile, solving ambiguity. So
From the pneumonia of the ditch, from the ague
Of the blind poet and the bombed-out town you bring
The all-clear to the empty holes of spring,
Rinsing the choked mud, keeping the colours new.

The Death of Marilyn Monroe

If it were said, let there be no more light,
Let rule the wide winds and the long-tailed seas,
Then she would die in all our hearts tonight—
Till when, her image broods over the cities
In negative, for the darkness she is bright,
Caught in a pose of infinite striptease.

Goddesses, from the whipped sea or the slums,
Will understand her final desolate
Stark-nakedness, her teeth ground to the gums,
Fingernails filthy, siren hair in spate
(And always with her, as she goes and comes,
Her little bottle of barbiturate)—

For she was one of them, queen among the trash,
Cinders swept to the palace from her shack
By some fairy godmother. In a flash
Spirited to the front row from the back.
Stars last so long before they go scattering ash
Down the cold back-streets of the zodiac—

Fall and dissolve into the thickening air,
Burning the black ground of the negative.
We are slowly learning from meteors like her
Who have learnt how to shrivel and let live,
That when an immovable body meets an ir-
Resistible force, something has got to give.

An Unborn Child

I have already come to the verge of
Departure. A month or so and
I shall be vacating this familiar room.
Its fabric fits me almost like a glove
While leaving latitude for a free hand.
I begin to put on the manners of the world,
Sensing the splitting light above
My head, where in the silence I lie curled.

Certain mysteries are relayed to me
Through the dark network of my mother's body
While she sits sewing the white shrouds
Of my apotheosis. I know the twisted
Kitten that lies there sunning itself
Under the bare bulb, the clouds
Of goldfish mooning around upon the shelf—
In me these data are already vested.

I feel them in my bones—bones which embrace
Nothing, for I am completely egocentric.
The pandemonium of encumbrances
Which will absorb me, mind and senses—
Intricacies of the box and the rat-race—
I imagine only. Though they linger and,
Like fingers, stretch until the knuckles crack,
They cannot dwarf the dimensions of my hand.

I must compose myself in the nerve-centre
Of this metropolis, and not fidget—
Although sometimes at night, when the city
Has gone to sleep, I keep in touch with it
Listening to the warm red water
Racing in the sewers of my mother's body—
Or the moths, soft as eyelids, or the rain
Wiping its wet wings on the window-pane.

And sometimes too, in the small hours of the morning
When the dead filament has ceased to ring—
After the goldfish are dissolved in darkness
And the kitten has gathered itself up into a ball
Between the groceries and the sewing,
I slip the trappings of my harness
To range these hollows in discreet rehearsal
And, battering at the concavity of my caul,

Produce in my mouth the words I WANT TO LIVE—
This my first protest, and shall be my last.
As I am innocent, everything I do
Or say is couched in the affirmative.
I want to see, hear, touch and taste
These things with which I am to be encumbered.
Perhaps I need not worry—give
Or take a day or two, my days are numbered.

In Belfast

Walking among my own this windy morning
In a tide of sunlight between shower and shower,
I resume my old conspiracy with the wet
Stone and the unwieldy images of the squinting heart.
Once more, as before, I remember not to forget.

There is a perverse pride in being on the side
Of the fallen angels and refusing to get up.
We could *all* be saved by keeping an eye on the hill
At the top of every street, for there it is—
Eternally, if irrelevantly, visible—

But yield instead to the humorous formulae,
The spurious mystery in the knowing nod.
Or we keep sullen silence in light and shade,
Rehearsing our astute salvations under
The cold gaze of a sanctimonious God.

One part of my mind must learn to know its place—
The things that happen in the kitchen-houses
And echoing back-streets of this desperate city
Should engage more than my casual interest,
Exact more interest than my casual pity.

Ecclesiastes

God, you could grow to love it, God-fearing, God-
    chosen purist little puritan that,
for all your wiles and smiles, you are (the
    dank churches, the empty streets,
the shipyard silence, the tied-up swings) and
    shelter your cold heart from the heat
of the world, from woman-inquisition, from the
    bright eyes of children. Yes you could
wear black, drink water, nourish a fierce zeal
    with locusts and wild honey, and not
feel called upon to understand and forgive
    but only to speak with a bleak
afflatus, and love the January rains when they
    darken the dark doors and sink hard
into the Antrim hills, the bog-meadows, the heaped
    graves of your fathers. Bury that red
bandana and stick, that banjo, this is your
    country, close one eye and be king.

Your people await you, their heavy washing
    flaps for you in the housing estates—
a credulous people. God, you could do it, God
    help you, stand on a corner stiff
with rhetoric, promising nothing under the sun.

The Snow Party
for Louis Asekoff

Bashō, coming
To the city of Nagoya,
Is asked to a snow party.

There is a tinkling of china
And tea into china,
There are introductions.

Then everyone
Crowds to the window
To watch the falling snow.

Snow is falling on Nagoya
And farther south
On the tiles of Kyōto.

Eastward, beyond Irago,
It is falling
Like leaves on the cold sea.

Elsewhere they are burning
Witches and heretics
In the boiling squares,

Thousands have died since dawn
In the service
Of barbarous kings—

But there is silence
In the houses of Nagoya
And the hills of Ise.

As It Should Be

We hunted the mad bastard
Through bog, moorland, rock, to the starlit west
And gunned him down in a blind yard
Between ten sleeping lorries
And an electricity generator.

Let us hear no idle talk
Of the moon in the Yellow River;
The air blows softer since his departure.

Since his tide-burial during school-hours
Our kiddies have known no bad dreams.
Their cries echo lightly along the coast.

This is as it should be.
They will thank us for it when they grow up
To a world with method in it.

Day Trip to Donegal
for Paul Smyth

We reached the sea in early afternoon,
Climbed stiffly out. There were urgent things to be done—
Clothes to be picked up, people to be seen.
As ever, the nearby hills were a deeper green
Than anywhere in the world, and the grave
Grey of the sea the grimmer in that enclave.

Down at the pier the boats gave up their catch—
Torn mouths and spewed-up lungs. They fetch
Ten times as much in the city as there,
And still the fish come in year after year—
Herring and whiting, flopping about the deck
In attitudes of agony and heartbreak.

We left at eight, drove back the way we came,
The sea receding down each muddy lane.
Around midnight we changed-down into suburbs
Sunk in a sleep no gale-force wind disturbs.
The time of year had left its mark
On frosty pavements glistening in the dark.

Give me a ring, goodnight, and so to bed...
That night the slow sea washed against my head,
Performing its immeasurable erosions—
Spilling into the skull, marbling the stones
That spine the very harbour wall,
Uttering its threat to villages of landfall.

At dawn I was alone far out at sea
Without skill or reassurance (nobody
To show me how, no earnest of rescue),
Cursing my mindless failure to take due
Forethought for this, contriving vain
Overtures to the mindless wind and rain.

Poem Beginning With a Line by Cavafy

It is night
And the barbarians have not come.
It was not always so hard;
When the great court flared
With gallowglasses and language difficulty
A man could be a wheelwright and die happy.

We remember
Oatmeal and mutton,
Harpsong, a fern table for
Wiping your hands on,
A candle of reeds and butter,
The distaste of the rheumatic chronicler,

A barbarous tongue
And herds like cloud-shadow
Roaming the wet hills
When the hills were young,
Whiskery pikemen and their spiky dogs
Preserved in woodcuts and card-catalogues.

Now it is night
And the barbarians have not come.
Or if they have we only recognize,
Harsh as a bombed bathroom,
The frantic anthropologisms
And lazarous ironies

Behind their talk
Of fitted carpets, central
Heating and automatic gear-change—
Like the bleached bones of a hare
Or a handful of spent
Cartridges on a deserted rifle range.

As God is My Judge

    They said I got away in a boat
And humbled me at the inquiry. I tell you
    I sank as far that night as any
Hero. As I sat shivering on the dark water
    I turned to ice to hear my costly
Life go thundering down in a pandemonium of
    Prams, pianos, sideboards, winches,
Boilers bursting and shredded ragtime. Now I hide
    In a lonely house behind the sea
Where the tide leaves broken toys and hatboxes
    Silently at my door. The showers of
April, flowers of May mean nothing to me, nor the
    Late light of June, when my gardener
Describes to strangers how the old man keeps his bed
    On seaward mornings after nights of
Wind, and will see no one, repeat no one. Then it is
    I drown again with all those dim
Lost faces I never understood. My poor soul
    Screams out in the starlight, heart
Breaks loose and rolls down like a stone. Include me
    Honoris causa in your lamentations.

BRUCE ISMAY

Gipsies Revisited
for Julian Harvey

I have watched the dark police
rocking your caravans
to wreck the crockery
and wry thoughts of peace
you keep there on waste
ground beside motorways
where the snow lies late
and am ashamed—fed,
clothed, housed and ashamed.
You might be interested
to hear, though, that on
stormy nights our strong
double glazing groans with
foreknowledge of death,
the fridge with a great wound,
and not surprised to know
the fate you have so long
endured is ours also,
the cars are piling up.
I listen to the wind
and file receipts. The heap
of scrap metal in my
garden grows daily.

A Disused Shed in Co. Wexford

Let them not forget us, the weak souls among the asphodels.
Seferis, *Mythistorema*

for J. G. Farrell

Even now there are places where a thought might grow—
Peruvian mines, worked out and abandoned
To a slow clock of condensation,
An echo trapped for ever, and a flutter of
Wildflowers in the lift-shaft,
Indian compounds where the wind dances
And a door bangs with diminished confidence,
Lime crevices behind rippling rainbarrels,
Dog corners for bone burials;
And in a disused shed in Co. Wexford,

Deep in the grounds of a burnt-out hotel,
Among the bathtubs and the washbasins
A thousand mushrooms crowd to a keyhole.
This is the one star in their firmament
Or frames a star within a star.
What should they do there but desire?
So many days beyond the rhododendrons
With the world waltzing in its bowl of cloud,
They have learnt patience and silence
Listening to the rooks querulous in the high wood.

They have been waiting for us in a foetor of
Vegetable sweat since civil war days,
Since the gravel-crunching, interminable departure
Of the expropriated mycologist.
He never came back, and light since then
Is a keyhole rusting gently after rain.
Spiders have spun, flies dusted to mildew,
And once a day, perhaps, they have heard something—
A trickle of masonry, a shout from the blue
Or a lorry changing gear at the end of the lane.

There have been deaths, the pale flesh flaking
Into the earth that nourished it;
And nightmares, born of these and the grim
Dominion of stale air and rank moisture.
Those nearest the door grow strong—
Elbow room! Elbow room!
The rest, dim in a twilight of crumbling
Utensils and broken pitchers, groaning
For their deliverance, have been so long
Expectant that there is left only the posture.

A half century, without visitors, in the dark—
Poor preparation for the cracking lock
And creak of hinges. Magi, moonmen,
Powdery prisoners of the old regime,
Web-throated, stalked like triffids, racked by drouth
And insomnia, only the ghost of a scream
At the flash-bulb firing squad we wake them with
Shows there is life yet in their feverish forms.
Grown beyond nature now, soft food for worms,
They lift frail heads in gravity and good faith.

They are begging us, you see, in their wordless way,
To do something, to speak on their behalf
Or at least not to close the door again.
Lost people of Treblinka and Pompeii!
Save us, save us, they seem to say,
Let the god not abandon us
Who have come so far in darkness and in pain.
We too had our lives to live.
You with your light meter and relaxed itinerary,
Let not our naive labours have been in vain!

TOM MATTHEWS b. 1945

Private But Sulphurous

My time he said was not my own
I had so much to do I was up at dawn

What with relations and friends
    and friends of relations
In the end they simply exhausted my patience

No more, I said to them all one day
No more for now, I am going on holiday
I wasn't of course, I was going away to stay

And I built this villa on Vesuvius
It is private here but sulphurous

Happy Arabia

'I speak for the world of scholarship'
    he said
'For knowledge for knowledge's sake'

And when the poet clutched his ankle
And murmured in delirium of Eden
He delivered him a lecture on its etymology

The poet heard only the words
Arabia Eudaimon
Arabia Felix
Happy Arabia

Oh happy happy happy Arabia

Robert Sat

The congregation was scandalised
When Robert sat in his pew and read a paperback

My mother said afterwards
'If he wasn't interested why did he come'

And I marvelled at her
For she never thought of applying that criterion
   to me

And I marvelled at Robert too
Able to read so calmly in the midst of so much
   hate

Robert is now doing very nicely thank you
He emigrated to Canada
And broke both legs in a skiing accident
And married a nurse

Cowboy Film

When asked her opinion
The old lady said

The horses were wrong
You never saw a white horse

And the children's teeth were wrong
Children had rotten teeth in those days

And the women were very wrong

Another thing she said was the smell
But you cannot expect films to smell

Even the Whales

Even the whales now
communicate sparingly with staccato cries
Polyphony was yesterday's song
We are minimalists
now, even the whales.

MICHAEL FOLEY b. 1947

from True Life Love Stories

16

Sois sage, ô ma doleur ... I don't
  hate the young anymore.
Let them greet with satirical
  signs of the cross

and smirk of their 'impecunious state'.
  I won't hate them
anymore. Love's the boyo to
  see them all straight,

so I muse, for I'm soft as an
  inside leg this year
all due to woman's passive power.
  Entends, ma chère,

this song and soft clip-clop is me.
  It's you I trot to,
tired and tame, melodious with
  new-found gallantry.

19

The sword is a cold bride. Yuk!
  I need the warmth
of fragrant human flesh (though I
  wouldn't deny our

good times on the march—untainted
  self-reliant band).
Ah comrades, it is time to say goodbye.
  If you could see

her you would understand. *She is*
  beautiful then? Yes
she is beautiful. Sad sighs and
  nods. We file outside,

still hushed observe the ancient soothing
   stars. *She will await*
you. Go to her. Firm Roman hand-
   shakes all round.

29
Ah no, ah no, they weren't all gross and slow.
   The message didn't
just read GO. There were many amusing
   men in that land—

they'd mostly failed but there it's
   what a man must do.
It's not the place for enterprise
   (their have-a-go grocer

got his head blown off). I'll miss its
   forty shades of spleen,
slouching off with my own, un-
   repentant churl.

It's *an honour* to merit
   the 'misfit' tag—
A felon's cap's the finest crown
   an Irish head can wear.

Lucky Eugene

a teaching poem

And the graduates can't stand the college-trained staff.
And the college-trained staff have their own way to scoff:

They expect a piece of paper to see them through.
But they both despise the lab. tech.—though it's due

To 'professional standing' and not a mere whim.
Choicer professions can't stand them. They can't stand him.

Eugene's the lab. technician. He's a non-staff grade
And that means no staff room for Eugene, I'm afraid!

NO markers of homework sharing funny mistakes.
NO epic anecdoters fouling coffee breaks.

NO dangerous after-schoolers wild with work-itch
(Lay their poor bones to rest in the all-weather pitch).

NO daddy-mad teasers, so hateful and thrilling
('Risk it for a biscuit'. 'Willing for a shilling'.)

And NO teachers' jargon—(the boss not a 'slob'
But 'a one-ulcer man in a two-ulcer job'.)

Lucky Eugene locked in the lab. beyond dislike
Blasting through The Decline and Fall of the Third Reich!

It's a bad scene, Euge, unromantic on the blurb
And as far as you can get from DO NOT DISTURB.

The Dance of Thought

What if you've nothing left to say?
What if your plans have come to naught?
There's nothing they can take away,
Your life is what you think all day,
  Dance the dance of thought!

What if you're never brash or bold?
What if you're feeling truly caught?
There's no way they can get a hold,
Salads in summer, stews for the cold,
  Dance the dance of thought!

What if your enemies get away?
What of the cutting edge you sought?
Satire and scorn have had their day.
Let the pipes and fiddles play,
  Dance the dance of thought!

FRANK ORMSBY b. 1947

My Friend Havelock Ellis

My first formal lesson on sex I owe
To my mother. Those faded books she bought
At the auction—sixpence the dozen, tied
With a rough string—hid one volume more
Than she bargained for.
For months I harboured him, forbidden one,
Under the green song sheets from *Ireland's Own.*

He never made the bookshelf, even wrapped
In a brown jacket. Consulted daily
Under clumps of trees beyond the hedge
That foiled the window's eye, his lectures turned
Often on mysteries.
I questioned him again until content
He'd yielded all, tutor and confidant.

Even in those days I knew at heart
How much he bored me. The tadpole-diagrams
He labelled Sperm, and cross-sections of organs
Like the cuts in butchers' windows, were less
Than living.
Still I intoned with a determined bliss
Words like fallopian, ovum, uterus.

The real joy was having such a friend,
Sure to be frowned on were his presence known.
He fed my independence, served a need
The set texts neglected. Nothing left then
But to discard him;
Time for fresh schooling, lessons to begin
In the arms of my new friend, Rosita Quinn.

Winter Offerings

Mother, it pains me that I must confide
To verse these clarities. We're each alone.
Our speech gutters. More than marriage divides
Us. Each visit home
I measure distances and find them grown.

It's your own fault, really. My good at heart
You grasped the chances that would sunder us.
I'm glad you chose to play the dogged part,
Take on the opposition. Often I wonder
How you prevailed against that blunderbuss

My father. What-was-good-enough-for-him—
The peasant's caution rather than a ploy
To keep me tethered; but you saw how grim
The prospects. Trapped yourself, you rescued me
From lives I guess at. Then, how could I joy

In love so functional, how call it love
That hid and whispered in a tough concern
With Grants and Benefits? So, schooled above
You, I grew up to miss those transferred yearnings.
School's out, but now in retrospect I learn.

Discarded woman, shame is turning me
To wish you mornings, and a folding night
Whose dreams are gentle, sight enough to see
This late guest bowed with winter offerings
Who turns his face into your going light.

Moving In

The first act of love in a new house
Is not private. Loving each other
We are half-aware of door and mirror.
Our ecstasy includes the bedside chair,
The air from the landing.

Street-lamp and elm utter leaves on walls
As in no room ever. Theirs is the tongue
Our tongues join in translating. Their message
Is clear: tonight you cannot ignore
The world at the window.

So we love in the knowledge of a city
At a different angle. And sharing
Our bed with furniture and tree we claim
Their perspective, merging our lives here
In their established frame.

A Day in August

And still no stronger. Swathed in rugs he lingered
  Near to the windows, gauging distant hills.
Balked by the panes that promised light and flowers,
  The wasps were dying furiously on sills.

A doctor called. She walked him to the doorstep,
  Then sent the children out to gather cones
Under the trees beside the ruined churchyard.
  They romped, unheeding, in the tilted stones.

And now the wheels are turning. They impress
  Tracks that will not outlast the winter's rain.
The siren leaves a wash of emptiness.
  He is lost to the small farms, lane by lane.

Passing the Crematorium

Someone is leaving town as clean smoke
This summer morning, too much the drifter
Now to let us know — even if he could—
His destination. Who watched, perhaps, the trail
Of jets in skies another summer
May find already that he's half-way there;
Or thinned instead into a blacker air
The factories muster. Whatever fate
Our leisured thought contrives to fit his journey
Pales with our passing;
Diverts no longer than we take to cruise
Beyond that frail thread, seawards, this summer morning.

CIARAN CARSON b. 1948

An Early Bed

A bubble of damp
jaundiced the scrolled flowers
on the candy-stripe wallpaper.
To pass the time,
I counted the flawed petals,
each flecked angrily with red,
like father's face.

His voice unravelled from below
in disembodied phrases—
A child who struck his father,
he once told me, died
soon afterwards;
but the disobedient hand
would not be buried:

One white flower
in a grave of flowers, it struggled
upwards through the clay
as if to fend off judgment.
I thought of dying out of spite,
my parents' faces worn
to a threadbare lace...

I held my breath
and tried to sink below the surface
of myself, into somewhere else.
But my right hand stayed where it was,
the final speck of air
blossoming above my finger.
I cried because I could not die.

This evening, re-papering
my room, those early failures
came to light. Tissued layers
peeled beneath the decorating knife
like fronds of skin. Beneath,
 gauzed over with old paste,
I found the yellowed flowers again.

Fishes in a Chinese Restaurant

I wonder if they see me.
Fluttering like swallows
Behind a window, their wings
Take the invisible

Curtain of water
Heavily as silk, as air
Before a storm, for their
Own weathers move them only

Slowly, their mouths opening
And shutting like an eyelid.
The branches where they nest
Half-asleep are those of

An ornamental garden;
Where they drift,
Miniature trees
Flower as paint through water;

The thin bubbles
Rising in scales to the surface
Mime various bird-musics.
Suddenly I felt helpless

As if, seeing an accident
Outside, my mouth was pressed
To the glass, my hands uttered
Dialects of silence.

The New Estate

Forget the corncrake's elegy. Rusty
Iambics that escaped your discipline
Of shorn lawns, it is sustained by nature.
It does not grieve for you, nor for itself.
You remember the rolled gold of cornfields,
Their rustling of tinsel in the wind,
A whole field quivering like blown silk?

A shiver now runs through the laurel hedge,
And washing flutters like the swaying lines
Of a new verse. The high fidelity
Music of the newly-wed obscures your
Dedication to a life of loving
Money. What could they be for, those marble
Toilet fixtures, the silence of water-beds,
That book of poems you bought yesterday?

The Bomb Disposal

Is it just like picking a lock
with the slow deliberation of a funeral,
hesitating through a darkened nave
until you find the answer?

Listening to the malevolent tick
of its heart, can you read
the message of the threaded veins
like print, its body's chart?

The city is a map of the city,
its forbidden areas changing daily.
I find myself in a crowded taxi
making deviations from the known route,

ending in a cul-de-sac
where everyone breaks out suddenly
in whispers, noting the boarded windows,
the drawn blinds.

The Car Cemetery

On winter nights
the cars bring in snow from the hills,
their bonnets white
above a wide cold smile of chromium.

From miles away
I see you coming in, a distant star
gone out of line, swaying
down from the road to take the thin lane

towards the house,
till my warm light and your cold are married,
your solitary noise
is lost among the rushing of the wind.

All around the world
there is a graveyard of defunct bodies,
wide smiles curled
in sleep. The cars at every door are hushed

beneath a soft corrosion
robed in white, these brides of silence
whose heaven
is like ours, a detritus of lights.

TOM PAULIN b. 1949

Settlers

They cross from Glasgow to a black city
    Of gantries, mills and steeples. They begin to belong.
He manages the Iceworks, is an elder of the Kirk;
    She becomes, briefly, a cook in Carson's Army.
Some mornings, walking through the company gate,
    He touches the bonnet of a brown lorry.
It is warm. The men watch and say nothing.
    'Queer, how it runs off in the night,'
He says to McCullough, then climbs to his office.
    He stores a warm knowledge on his palm.

Nightlandings on the Antrim coast, the movement of guns
    Now snug in their oiled paper below the floors
Of sundry kirks and tabernacles in that county.

Under the Eyes

Its retributions work like clockwork
Along murdering miles of terrace-houses
Where someone is saying, 'I am angry,
I am frightened, I am justified.
Every favour, I must repay with interest,
Any slight against myself, the least slip,
Must be balanced out by an exact revenge.'

The city is built on mud and wrath.
Its weather is predicted; its streetlamps
Light up in the glowering, crowded evenings.
Time-switches, ripped from them, are clamped
To sticks of sweet, sweating explosive.
All the machinery of a state
Is a set of scales that squeezes out blood.

Memory is just, too. A complete system
Nothing can surprise. The dead are recalled
From schoolroom afternoons, the hill quarries
Echoing blasts over the secured city;
Or, in a private house, a Judge
Shot in his hallway before his daughter
By a boy who shut his eyes as his hand tightened.

A rain of turds; a pair of eyes; the sky and tears.

A New Society

It's easy enough to regret them when they're gone.
Beds creaked on boards in the brick meadows
Somewhere above a tired earth no one had seen
Since Arkwright became a street name.

Their boxed rooms were papered with generations,
There were gas lamps, corner shops that smelt of wrapped bread,
Worn thresholds warmed by the sun and kids playing ball
Near the odd, black, Ford Popular.

Then they were empty like plague streets, their doors barred
And windows zinced. Dead lids weighted with coins,
Dead ends all of them when their families left.
Then broken terraces carried away in skips.

A man squints down a theodolite, others stretch white tapes
Over the humped soil or dig trenches that are like useful graves.
Diesel combusts as yellow bulldozers push earth
With their shields. Piledrivers thud on open ground.

Just watching this—the laid-out streets, the mixers
Churning cement, the new bricks rising on their foundations—
Makes me want to believe in some undoctrinaire
Statement of what should be. A factual idealism.

A mummified Bentham should flourish in this soil
And unfold an order that's unaggressively civilian,
Where taps gush water into stainless sinks
And there's a smell of fresh paint in sunlit kitchens.

Where rats are destroyed and crawlies discouraged,
Where the Law is glimpsed on occasional traffic duties
And the streets are friendly with surprise recognitions.
Where, besides these, there's a visible water

That lets the sun dazzle on Bank Holidays, and where kids
Can paddle safely. There should be some grass, too,
And the chance of an unremarkable privacy,
A vegetable silence there for the taking.

Monumental Mason

Working beside a cemetery,
Chiselling dates and names
On cheap slabs of marble
In the lighted shop window,
His meek power makes us nervous.

With his back to the street,
He cuts them in, these loves
The dead can't care about.
In his washed-out overalls
He is less a person

Than a function. People
Have grown used to him
As he sits intently
Gilding the incised letters,
A mason, displayed.

Doris, Beloved Wife
And Mother, or *Agnes*
RIP, their names are
Public, but we forget them,
Glimpsing a tenderness

On bald stone, some dead letters;
Or, when the traffic lulls,
Hearing from next door
The undertaker's tap, tap,
Answer his vigilant chinking.

Deceased Effects

We go to auctions now and bid for things
That people once belonged to. They've shed their lives
And kept a dust that never quite scrubs off.
Unfaithful survivors, they fall to scruffy dealers,
The poor, or the ambitious young. Quaint now,
The functional metal beds the dead once woke in
When sirens went at five and mills clanked all night.

Those little bits of china that were fixed
To mantelshelves in neat front rooms, the chairs
They sat in, all the odds and ends they lived among.
Parts of a pattern that only seemed to fit,
Tell us nothing and never go for much—
Though last week there was one lot that told
Its own sparse story: a pile of photographs,
The wedding sometime, plain, unfashionable,
Six fresh-faced children behind dusty glass,
The couple older on an anniversary, and then,
Almost too pat, a mountain of wreaths on a grave,
Knocked down to someone for the frames.

PAUL MULDOON b. 1951

Dancers at the Moy

This Italian square
And circling plain
Black once with mares
And their stallions,
The flat Blackwater
Turning its stones

Over hour after hour
As their hooves shone
And lifted together
Under the black rain,
One or other Greek war
Now coloured the town

Blacker than ever before
With hungry stallions
And their hungry mares
Like hammocks of skin,
The flat Blackwater
Unable to contain

Itself as horses poured
Over acres of grain
In a black and gold river.
No band of Athenians
Arrived at the Moy fair
To buy for their campaign,

Peace having been declared
And a treaty signed.
The black and gold river
Ended as a trickle of brown
Where those horses tore
At briars and whins,

Ate the flesh of each other
Like people in famine.
The flat Blackwater
Hobbled on its stones
With a wild stagger
And sag in its backbone,

The local people gathered
Up the white skeletons.
Horses buried for years
Under the foundations
Give their earthen floors
The ease of trampolines.

The Field Hospital

Taking, giving back their lives
By the strength of our bare hands,
By the silence of our knives,
We answer to no grey South

Nor blue North, not self defence,
The lie of just wars, neither
Cold nor hot blood's difference
In their discharging of guns,

But that hillside of fresh graves.
Would this girl brought to our tents
From whose flesh we have removed
Shot that George, on his day off,

Will use to weight fishing lines,
Who died screaming for ether,
Yet protest our innocence?
George lit the lanterns, in danced

Those gigantic yellow moths
That brushed right over her wounds,
Pinning themselves to our sleeves
Like medals given the brave.

The Centaurs

I can think of William of Orange,
Prince of gasworks-wall and gable-end.
A plodding, snow-white charger
On the green, grassy slopes of the Boyne,
The milk-cart swimming against the current

Of our own backstreet. Hernan Cortes
Is mustering his cavalcade on the pavement,
Lifting his shield like the lid of a garbage-can.
His eyes are fixed on a river of Aztec silver,
He whinnies and paws the earth

For our amazement. And Saul of Tarsus,
The stone he picked up once has grown into a hoof.
He slings the saddle-bags over his haunches,
Lengthening his reins, loosening his girth,
To thunder down the long road to Damascus.

The Merman

He was ploughing his single furrow
Through the green, heavy sward
Of water. I was sowing winter wheat
At the shoreline, when our farms met.

Not a furrow, quite, I argued.
Nothing would come of his long acre
But breaker growing out of breaker,
The wind-scythe, the rain-harrow.

Had he no wish to own such land
As he might plough round in a day?
What of friendship, love? Such qualities?

He remembered these same fields of corn or hay
When swathes ran high along the ground,
Hearing the cries of one in difficulties.

Duffy's Circus

Once Duffy's Circus had shaken out its tent
In the big field near the Moy
God may as well have left Ireland
And gone up a tree. My father had said so.

There was no such thing as the five-legged calf,
The God of Creation
Was the God of Love.
My father chose to share such Nuts of Wisdom.

Yet across the Alps of each other the elephants
Trooped. Nor did it matter
When Wild Bill's Rain Dance
Fell flat. Some clown emptied a bucket of stars

Over the swankiest part of the crowd.
I had lost my father in the rush and slipped
Out the back. Now I heard
For the first time that long-drawn-out cry.

It came from somewhere beyond the corral.
A dwarf on stilts. Another dwarf.
I sidled past some trucks. From under a freighter
I watched a man sawing a woman in half.

Wind and Tree

In the way that the most of the wind
Happens where there are trees,

Most of the world is centred
About ourselves.

Often where the wind has gathered
The trees together and together,

One tree will take
Another in her arms and hold.

Their branches that are grinding
Madly together and together,

It is no real fire.
They are breaking each other.

Often I think I should be like
The single tree, going nowhere,

Since my own arm could not and would not
Break the other. Yet by my broken bones

I tell new weather.

The Mixed Marriage

My father was a servant-boy.
When he left school at eight or nine
He took up billhook and loy
To win the ground he would never own.

My mother was the school-mistress,
The world of Castor and Pollux.
There were twins in her own class.
She could never tell which was which.

She had read one volume of Proust,
He knew the cure for farcy.
I flitted between a hole in the hedge
And a room in the Latin Quarter.

When she had cleared the supper-table
She opened *The Acts of the Apostles*,
Aesop's Fables, Gulliver's Travels.
Then my mother went on upstairs

And my father further dimmed the light
To get back to hunting with ferrets
Or the factions of the faction-fights,
The Ribbon Boys, the Caravats.

Ma

Old photographs would have her bookish, sitting
Under a willow. I take that to be a croquet
Lawn. She reads aloud, no doubt from Rupert Brooke.
The month is always May or June.

Or with the stranger on the motor-bike.
Not my father, no. This one's all crew-cut
And polished brass buttons.
An American soldier, perhaps.
                              And the full moon
Swaying over Keenaghan, the orchards and the cannery,
Thins to a last yellow-hammer, and goes.
The neighbours gather, all Keenaghan and Collegelands,
There is story-telling. Old miners at Coalisland
Going into the ground. Swinging, for fear of the gas,
The soft flame of a canary.

GERALD DAWE b.1952

Bloody Foreland
for Christabel Bielenberg

No man could stand here long
where the Atlantic rises up
and the Foreland hangs across...

the huge stones rumble:
there is only one life here
watching and knowing
like the gull
hovering and screaming,
to plunge
and glide
and cry again
that shrill pitch
like widows' keening...

once, in the city,
sauntered into
the wrong kitchen-house,
them all in black
in a dark parlour
baying to the moon
an archaic death...

the stones applaud.
You cannot turn
and walk and speak
of our past
        as something
natural.

Pauper and Poet

The ways out have changed
but not the facts of going.
Before, they gathered along
morning shores and waited
for the heavy ships to
weigh in.
      Then it was
a necessity rooted
in stinking land, hope-
less crops that weaned
a new generation
to hope: memories
tarred with despair.
You couldn't live there.
      And others
set sail, desperate
for revenge, sat
in civilised houses
and wrote till famous—
their plight fed
on images of the dead.
They weren't among the dying.

Sheltering Places
for Norma Fitzgerald

It's been pelting down
all night the kind
of rain that drenches
to the bone

and a dirtstorm
in the car park.
The hot wind carries
thunder making girls

204

scream and old men
count the seconds,
improvising distance
as you shout to

turn the lights out
pull down the blinds
so that lightning can't
get in and frazzle us up

in the curtain-dark room
the rumbles near and
shattering flashes
make everything go numb.

The storm is reaching
home territory, stretching
over the hills down
into our sheltering places.

Physical Environment

We grew out of sloblands
when the ice-pack shrank

we walk upon a river
that runs underneath streets

a haemorrhaged vein
pumping bad blood

our city suffers its
blackheart houses

wastelands grown from
a century's worth

of tenement men
sniffing dock poison

skin gets livid white
till words come like

those a sick man speaks:
we've grown to live with it.

Names

They call this 'Black North'
black from the heart out—

it doesn't matter about
particularities when mouths

mumble the handy sayings
and day-in minds tighten.

I've been here having thought
nowhere else was possible,

a condition of destiny or what
the old generations only fumbled

with: conceit, success, a fair
share of decent hardship,

compounded, forced into fierce
recognition—the cardhouse toppled.

In this extreme, perched
on the edge of the Atlantic

you feel to look down
and gather around the details

thinking to store them away
bundle and pack in the exile's way—

the faithful journey
of turning your back

like the host of others
the scholars and saints.

Line up and through the turn-
stile, click the ticket

and wait till you're
clear of it: glued to

the passport: IRISH POET,
Destination, America or

Early Grave. You need never
recall the other names.

WILLIAM PESKETT b. 1952

The Question of Time

Where on earth
has the stumbling mammoth gone?
that giant tripper over nations
who used to think
the world was his
after the succulent brontosaurus.

The ages shed no tears for me.
I am not their resting
but their passing through,
left to watch
the intricate bees
in their noble art of dance.

Star and Sea

That star I now see
blended in the night's bright telegraph
has long since burnt out
and exploded.
The slowness of its fumes of light
across space provides
a second's vision of the past.
Gleeful time-traveller,
I forget I'm divided from a truth.

Cold water from the south
melts sombre
from the brilliant cap.
The slow currents north
take seven years to chill me,
to reach me with their dated clutter
from the ocean floor—time enough
for sea-change, a skin-change;
a new man reading old news.

The Inheritors
for Paul Muldoon

And the ones that got tough
ripped the soft parts
from the sea.
With a spine and a jaw
they pressed a clear advantage,
picking bones with ones
whose shadows met their own.
Gasping, they broke the surface.

The ones that had legs
came up where there was nothing.
Starting as one,
they split into bands
and savaged the green ground.
Ambivalent, they slid in the swamp
from home to home, cleverer,
keeping their options open.

The ones that could crawl
stood up and dried
the afterbirth from their backs.
Somehow they grew to break
the treaty of the land:
becoming gross they tore
the flesh of the sinless
and took three elements in their stride.

The ones that were feathered
came to know the slaughter
of the plain. Gliding from cliffs
they tumbled to the line of flight.
Innocent in the air, their shapes
against the sun began to drop—
below, their claws ripped fur
from nervous carcasses.

And the ones that gave suck
ran like warm blood
through high branches.
With a crib for their young
their lives might have been maternal
but for precedent. Not born
to run with the innocent,
inheritors, we kill.

Bottles in the Zoological Museum

Bottles are for sleeping in—
they exorcise you
giving a live and pink
fluorescence to your skin.

Bottles contain you,
sinless and dreamless
you sink in their liquid
as eiderdown.

There are never men
in bottles—only animals
and babies and half-babies,
their softness gritting.

No man is accepted here.
I see a foetus crouch,
not in attack
but discovery of other shelves.

Window Dressing

The beautiful man and his wife
must have fled,
deserting their immaculate husks
like wholesome insects
on a jagged flight to a new life.

The copies that remain possess everything.
In their still and vigilant life
of display they need cocktail cabinets
and sofas
but have no inclination to move over,

to touch and merge.
The actual people, lush and naked,
are hovering on transient wings:
they're making love
out of hours.

On dark nights, through the window
on their brilliant home
I see them returning,
sheepish and ashamed,
slipping back into shape.

Biographical and
Bibliographical Notes

GEORGE BUCHANAN

b. 1904 in Kilwaughter, Larne, Co Antrim. Educated Larne Grammar School and Campbell College, Belfast. Worked as a journalist on various Irish and English newspapers, including *The Times*. Joined RAF in 1940. Chairman Town and Country Development Committee, NI, 1949-53. He has published two journals, two volumes of autobiography, six novels and a book of essays and has had a number of plays produced.

By George Buchanan:
Bodily Responses. Poems. Gaberbocchus, 1958.
Conversation With Strangers. Poems. Gaberbocchus, 1961.
Annotations. Poems. Carcanet Press, 1970.
Minute-Book of a City. Poems. Carcanet, 1972.
Inside Traffic. Poems. Carcanet, 1976.
Green Seacoast. Autobiography, Gaberbocchus, 1959.
Morning Papers. Autobiography. Gaberbocchus, 1965.
The Politics of Culture. Essays. Menard Press, 1977.

About George Buchanan:
'George Buchanan: A Special Supplement' in *The Honest Ulsterman*, No 59, March/June 1978, pp 17-87. Includes an essay by James Simmons on Buchanan's poetry.

Recordings:
George Buchanan Reading His Poems. Cassette. Audio Arts, London, 1977.

JOHN HEWITT

b.1907 in Belfast. Educated Methodist College and Queen's University. On the staff of the Belfast Museum and Art Gallery, 1930-57. Art Director of the Herbert Art Gallery and Museum, Coventry, 1957-72. Editor and art critic, as well as poet. Has written monographs on the Ulster painters Colin Middleton and John Luke, been poetry editor of *Threshold* (1957-62) and edited selections of William Allingham's poems (Dolmen Press, 1967) and the verse of the Rhyming Weavers (Blackstaff Press, 1974). Also wrote *Art in Ulster I* (Blackstaff Press), an account of four centuries of Ulster painting, drawing, prints and sculpture up until 1957. Was Writer in Residence at Queen's University, 1976-79.

By John Hewitt:
No Rebel Word. Poems. Frederick Muller, 1948.
Collected Poems. MacGibbon and Kee, 1968.
Out of My Time. Poems. Blackstaff Press, 1974.
Time Enough. Poems. Blackstaff Press, 1976.
The Rain Dance. Poems. Blackstaff Press, 1978.
'No Rootless Colonist'. *Aquarius*, No 5, 1972, pp 90-95.

About John Hewitt:
Brown, Terence: 'John Hewitt: Land and People', in *Northern Voices. Poets From Ulster*, Gill and Macmillan, 1975, pp 86-97.
Foster, John Wilson: 'The Landscape of the Planter and the Gael in the Poetry of John Hewitt and John Montague', *Canadian Journal of Irish Studies*, Vol 1, No 2, Nov 1975, pp 17-33.
Grennan, Eamonn: Review article on Hewitt's *Out of my Time* and *Time Enough, Eire/Ireland*, Summer 1977, pp 143-51.
Heaney, Seamus: 'The Poetry of John Hewitt', *Threshold*, No 22, Summer 1969, pp 73-77.
Montague, John: 'Regionalism into Reconciliation: The Poetry of John Hewitt', *Poetry Ireland*, No 13, Spring 1964, pp 113-118.
Sealy, Douglas: 'An Individual Flavour: The Collected Poems of John Hewitt', *The Dublin Magazine*, Vol 8, Nos 1-2, Spring/Summer 1969, pp 19-24.

Film:
'I found Myself Alone'. Arts Council of Northern Ireland, 1978.

LOUIS MacNEICE
b.1907 in Belfast. Father became Rector of St Nicholas' Church, Carrickfergus in 1908. Mother died of tuberculosis in 1914. Attended Sherbourne Preparatory School in Dorset, 1917-21, and Marlborough College, Wiltshire, 1921-26. Read Classics and Philosophy at Oxford,

1926-30. Married and was appointed lecturer in Classics at Birmingham University in 1930. Divorced, 1936. First book of poems appeared in 1929 and he published regularly throughout the Thirties. Served as firewatcher in London, 1940. Joined BBC as scriptwriter and producer in 1941. Re-married in 1942 and continued to publish steadily — poetry, radio plays, translations, criticism. Died in 1963.

By Louis MacNeice:

Collected Poems. Faber, 1966. New edition, 1969. Paperback, 1979.
Selected Poems, ed. W. H. Auden. Faber, 1964.
Modern Poetry. A Personal Essay. Criticism. Oxford University Press, 1938.
The Strings Are False. Autobiography. Faber, 1965.
'Experiences With Images', *Orpheus*, Vol 2, 1949, pp 124-32.

About Louis MacNeice:

Allen, Walter: 'Louis MacNeice', in *Essays by Divers Hands*, Vol 35, 1969, pp 1-17.
Brown, Terence: *Louis MacNeice: Sceptical Vision.* Gill and Macmillan, 1975.
Brown, Terence and Reid, Alec ed.: *Time Was Away: The World of Louis MacNeice.* Dolmen Press, 1974.
Fraser, G.S.: 'Evasive Honesty', in *Vision and Rhetoric.* Faber, 1959, pp 193-201.
Hamilton, Ian: 'Louis MacNeice', in *A Poetry Chronicle.* Faber, 1973, pp 30-36.
McKinnon, William T.: *Apollo's Blended Dream.* Oxford University Press, 1971.
Moore, D.B.: *The Poetry of Louis MacNeice.* Leicester University Press, 1972.
Press, John: *Louis MacNeice.* Longmans, Green and Co for the British Council, 1965.
Smith, Elton Edward: *Louis MacNeice.* Twayne Publishers, Inc., 1970.

Recordings:

Louis MacNeice Reads Selected Poems. Argo, London, 1961.

W. R. RODGERS

b.1909 in Belfast. Graduated from Queen's University in 1931. Ordained in 1935 and appointed Presbyterian minister at Loughgall, Co. Armagh. Married in 1936. Joined BBC in London in 1946. Married for second time in 1953. Lived at various times in Suffolk, Essex and California. Died in Los Angeles in 1969. Buried in Loughgall. Journalist and scriptwriter for radio, as well as poet.

By W. R. Rodgers:
Awake! and Other Poems. Secker and Warburg, 1941.
Europa and the Bull. Poems. Secker and Warburg, 1952.
Collected Poems. Oxford University Press, 1971.
'Conversation Piece by An Ulster Protestant', *The Bell*, Vol IV, No 5, Aug 1942, pp 305-14.
'Black North', *New Statesman and Nation*, 20 Nov, 1943, pp 331-32.
'Balloons and Maggots' *Rann*, No 14, 1951, pp 8-13.
'Time to Kill', *New Statesman and Nation*, 21 March, 1953, p 336.
'The Dance of Words', *New Statesman and Nation*, 1 Aug, 1953, p 126.

About W. R. Rodgers:
Amis, Kingsley: 'Ulster Bull: The Case of W. R. Rodgers', *Essays in Criticism*, Vol 3, No 4, Oct 1953, pp 470-75.
Brown, Terence: 'W. R. Rodgers: Romantic Calvinist', in *Northern Voices* pp 114-27.
O'Brien, Darcy: *W. R. Rodgers.* Bucknell University Press, 1970.

Recordings:
Europa and the Bull. W. R. Rodgers reading from his second volume. Argo, London, 1953/54.

ROY McFADDEN
b.1921 in Belfast, where he still practises as a solicitor. Emerged as a poet in the 1940s, during which he joint-edited the magazine *Rann* and the broadsheet *Ulster Voices* and was an associate editor of *Lagan*. First appeared in book form, with Alex Comfort and Ian Serraillier, in the anthology *Three New Poets*, Grey Walls Press, 1942.

By Roy McFadden:
Swords and Ploughshares. Poems. Routledge, 1943.
Flowers for a Lady. Poems. Routledge, 1945.
The Heart's Townland. Poems. Routledge, 1947.
Elegy for the Dead of the 'Princess Victoria'. Poem. Lisnagarvey Press, 1953.
The Garryowen. Poems. Chatto and Windus, 1971.
Verifications. Poems. Blackstaff Press, 1977.
A Watching Brief. Poems. Blackstaff Press, 1979.
'A Trend in Poetry', *The Dublin Magazine*, Oct-Dec, 1944, pp 43-48
'Conversation in a Shaving-Mirror', *Poetry Ireland*, No. 15, October 1951, pp 9-13.

About Roy McFadden:
Brown, Terence: 'Robert Greacen and Roy McFadden: Apocalypse and Survival', in *Northern Voices*, pp 128-40.

PADRAIC FIACC

b.1924 in Belfast. Family emigrated to New York, where Fiacc was educated at Commerce and Haaren High Schools, Manhattan and St Joseph's Seminary Calicoon, New York State. Returned to Belfast in 1946. Won the A.E. Memorial Award in 1947. Edited *The Wearing of the Black* (Blackstaff Press, 1974), an anthology of contemporary Ulster poetry.

By Padraic Fiacc:
By the Black Stream. Poems. Dolmen Press, 1969.
Odour of Blood. Poems. Goldsmith Press, 1973.
Nights in the Bad Place. Poems. Blackstaff Press, 1977.
The Selected Padraic Fiacc. Blackstaff Press, 1979.
About Padraic Fiacc:
Brown, Terence: 'Padraic Fiacc: The Bleeding Bough', in *Northern Voices*, pp 141-48.
Introduction to *The Selected Padraic Fiacc*. Blackstaff Press, 1979.

JOHN MONTAGUE

b.1929 in Brooklyn, New York, but in 1933 moved to Co Tyrone to live on his aunts' farm. Educated at St Patrick's College, Armagh and University College, Dublin. Studied and taught in the USA, 1953-56. Moved to Paris, 1961. Has lectured in University College, Cork since 1972. Editor of the *Faber Book of Irish Verse* (1974).

By John Montague:
Poisoned Lands. Poems. MacGibbon and Kee Ltd, 1961. Revised edition, Dolmen Press, 1977.
A Chosen Light. Poems. MacGibbon and Kee Ltd, 1967.
Tides. Poems. Dolmen Press, 1970.
The Rough Field. Poems. Dolmen Press, 1972.
A Slow Dance. Poems. Dolmen Press, 1975.
The Great Cloak, Poems. Dolmen Press, 1978.
Death of a Chieftain. Short Stories. MacGibbon & Kee Ltd, 1964. Re-issued by Poolbeg Press, 1978.
'The Rough Field', *The Spectator*, 26 April 1963, p 531.
'The Seamless Garment and the Muse', *Agenda*, Vol 5, No 4/Vol 6, No 1, Autumn/Winter, 1967-68.
'The Impact of International Modern Poetry on Irish Writing' in *Irish Poets in English*, ed Sean Lucy, Mercier Press, 1973, pp 144-58.

'In the Irish Grain'. Introduction to *Faber Book of Irish Verse*, 1974, pp 21-39.

About John Montague:

Brown Terence: 'John Montague: Circling to Return' in *Northern Voices*, pp 149-70.

Foster, John Wilson: 'The Landscape of the Planter and the Gael in the Poetry of John Hewitt and John Montague', *Canadian Journal of Irish Studies*, Vol 1, No 2, Nov 1975, pp 17-33.

Kersnowski, Frank: *John Montague*. Bucknell University Press, 1975.

Longley, Edna: 'Searching the Darkness: Richard Murphy, Thomas Kinsella, John Montague and James Simmons' in *Two Decades of Irish Writing. A Critical Survey* ed Douglas Dunn. Carcanet Press, 1975, pp 118-53.

Lucy, Sean: 'Three Poets From Ulster', *Irish University Review*, Vol 3, No 2, Autumn 1973, pp 179-93.

Maxwell, D.E.S.: 'The Poetry of John Montague', *Critical Quarterly*, Vol XV, No 2, Summer 1973, pp 180-185.

Redshaw, Thomas Dillon: 'John Montague's *The Rough Field*: Topos and Texne', Studies, Vol LXIII, Spring 1974, pp 31-46.

Recordings:

The Northern Muse. Seamus Heaney and John Montague reading their own poems. Claddagh Records, Dublin, 1968.

JAMES SIMMONS

b.1933 in Derry. Educated at Foyle College and Leeds University. Taught at Friends' School, Lisburn, for five years, and at Ahmadu Bello University, Zaria, Nigeria. Returned from Africa in 1967, founded *The Honest Ulsterman* the following year and edited the first nineteen numbers. Songwriter and singer as well as poet. Has issued two LPs, *City and Eastern* and *Love in the Post*. Won an Eric Gregory Award in 1961 and a Cholmondeley Award in 1977. Currently a Senior Lecturer in English at the New University of Ulster.

By James Simmons:

Late But in Earnest. Poems. Bodley Head, 1967.

In the Wilderness and Other Poems. Bodley Head, 1969.

Energy to Burn. Poems. Bodley Head, 1971.

No Land Is Waste, Dr. Eliot. Poems. Keepsake Press, 1972.

The Long Summer Still to Come. Poems. Blackstaff Press. 1973.

West Strand Visions. Poems. Blackstaff Press, 1974.

Judy Garland and the Cold War. Poems. Blackstaff Press, 1976.

The Selected James Simmons. Poems, ed. Edna Longley. Blackstaff Press, 1978.

About James Simmons:
Brown, Terence: 'Four New Voices: Poets of the Present' in *Northern Voices*, pp 171-213.
Longley, Edna: Introduction to *The Selected James Simmons*. Blackstaff Press, 1978.

SEAMUS HEANEY
b.1939 in Co Derry. Educated at St Columb's College and Queen's University, where he also lectured. Taught for a year at the University of California at Berkeley. Has won Eric Gregory (1966), Cholmondeley (1967), Somerset Maugham (1968), Denis Devlin (1972), American Irish Foundation (1972) and Duff Cooper Memorial (1975) Awards for his poetry. Now lives in Dublin and lectures at Carysfort College.

By Seamus Heaney:
Death of a Naturalist. Poems. Faber, 1966.
Door into the Dark. Poems. Faber, 1969.
Wintering Out. Poems. Faber, 1972.
North. Poems. Faber, 1975.

About Seamus Heaney:
Brown, Terence: 'Four New Voices: Poets of the Present' in *Northern Voices*, pp 171-213.
Buttel, Robert: *Seamus Heaney*. Bucknell University Press, 1975.
Foster, John Wilson: 'Seamus Heaney's "A Lough Neagh Sequence": Sources and Motifs', *Eire/Ireland*, Summer 1977, pp 138-42.
Maxwell, D.E.S.: 'Contemporary Poetry in the North of Ireland' in *Two Decades of Irish Writing*, edited by Douglas Dunn, Carcanet Press, 1975, pp 166-85.
McGuinness, Arthur E.: '"Hoarder of the Common Ground": Tradition and Ritual in Seamus Heaney's Poetry', *Eire/Ireland*, Summer 1978, pp 71-92.

Recordings:
The Northern Muse, with John Montague. Claddagh Records, Dublin, 1968.

MICHAEL LONGLEY
b.1939 in Belfast. Educated at the Royal Belfast Academical Institution and Trinity College, Dublin. Taught at RBAI for a time before joining the Arts Council of Northern Ireland, of which he is now an Assistant Director. Won an Eric Gregory Award in 1965. Has edited

Over the Moon and Under the Stars (Arts Council, 1971), an anthology of Ulster children's poetry, and *Causeway. The Arts in Ulster* (Arts Council, 1971).

By Michael Longley:
No Continuing City. Poems. Macmillan, 1969.
An Exploded View. Poems. Gollancz, 1973.
Man Lying on a Wall. Poems. Gollancz, 1976.

About Michael Longley:
Allen, Michael: 'Options: The Poetry of Michael Longley', *Eire/Ireland,* Winter 1975, pp 129-36.
Brown, Terence: *Northern Voices,* pp 171-213.
Maxwell, D.E.S.: *Two Decades of Irish Writing,* pp 166-85.

Recordings:
Words Alone. Michael Longley and Derek Mahon reading their own poems. Outlet Recordings, **Belfast, 1968.**

SEAMUS DEANE
b.1940 in Derry. Educated at St Columb's College and Queen's University. Taught in Derry and is now a lecturer in UCD. Has also lectured in America. Winner of the A.E. Memorial Award in 1973.

By Seamus Deane
Gradual Wars. Poems. Irish University Press, 1972.
Rumours. Poems. Dolmen Press, 1977.

DEREK MAHON
b.1941 in Belfast. Educated at the Royal Belfast Academical Institution and Trinity College, Dublin. Has worked as a teacher in Ireland, Canada and the USA and as a journalist. **Won an Eric Gregory Award in 1965 and has been Writer in Residence at the New** University of Ulster. Edited the *Sphere Book of Modern Irish Poetry* in 1972.

By Derek Mahon:
Night-Crossing. Poems. Oxford University Press, 1968.
Lives. Poems. Oxford University Press, 1972.
The Snow Party. Poems. Oxford University Press, 1975.

About Derek Mahon:
Brown, Terence: *Northern Voices*, pp 171-213.
Dunn, Douglas: 'Let the God Not Abandon Us: On the poetry of Derek Mahon.' *Stone Ferry Review*, No 2, Winter 1978, pp 7-30.
Maxwell, D.E.S.: *Two Decades of Irish Writing*, pp 166-85.

Recordings:
Words Alone with Michael Longley. Outlet Recordings, Belfast, 1968.
Derek Mahon reads his own poetry. Claddagh Records, Dublin, 1973.

TOM MATTHEWS
b.1945 in Ballymena, but brought up in Derry. Educated at Foyle College and Queen's University. Lives in Larne and works as a chemist in a cement works.

By Tom Matthews
Dr. Wilson as an Arab. Poems. Holysmoke Press, 1974.

MICHAEL FOLEY
b.1947 in Derry. Educated at St Columb's College and Queen's University, where he took a Science degree. Joint-edited *The Honest Ulsterman* with Frank Ormsby from 1969 to 1972. Teaches in London. His novel *The Life of Jamesie Coyle* has been serialised in the Belfast periodical, *Fortnight*.

By Michael Foley:
True Life Love Stories. Poems. Blackstaff Press, 1976.

FRANK ORMSBY
b.1947 in Enniskillen. Educated at St Michael's College and Queen's University. Has taught in the Royal Belfast Academical Institution since 1971. Won an Eric Gregory Award in 1974 and has been editor of *The Honest Ulsterman*, jointly or alone, since 1969.

By Frank Ormsby
A Store of Candles. Poems. Oxford University Press, 1977.

CIARAN CARSON
b.1948 in Belfast. His first language was Irish. After graduating from Queen's University he worked as a civil servant and teacher. Is

currently Traditional Arts Officer with the Arts Council. Won an Eric Gregory Award in 1978.

By Ciarán Carson
The New Estate. Poems. Blackstaff Press, 1976.

TOM PAULIN
b.1949 in Leeds but grew up in Belfast. Educated at Annadale Grammar School and the Universities of Hull and Oxford. Lectures in English at the University of Nottingham. Won an Eric Gregory Award in 1976 and a Somerset Maugham Award in 1978. His critical work, *Thomas Hardy: The Poetry of Perception*, was published by Macmillan in 1975.

By Tom Paulin:
A State of Justice. Poems. Faber, 1977.

PAUL MULDOON
b.1951 in Co Armagh. Grew up in The Moy, Co Tyrone. Educated at St Patrick's College, Armagh and Queen's University. Won an Eric Gregory Award in 1972. Works as a producer in the BBC in Belfast.

By Paul Muldoon:
New Weather. Poems. Faber, 1973.
Mules. Poems. Faber, 1977.

GERALD DAWE
b..1952 in Belfast. Educated at the New University of Ulster and University College, Galway, where he now tutors. Has worked with the Lyric Youth Theatre in Belfast and has written plays.

By Gerald Dawe:
Sheltering Places. Poems. Blackstaff Press, 1978.

WILLIAM PESKETT
b.1952 in Cambridge but came to Belfast in 1959. Educated at the Royal Belfast Academical Institution and Christ's College, Cambridge, where he read zoology. Co-edited the literary magazine *Caret*. Won an Eric Gregory Award in 1976. Teaches in England.

By William Peskett:
The Night-owl's Dissection. Poems. Secker and Warburg, 1975.

Bibliography

Bell, Sam Hanna: *The Theatre in Ulster*. Gill and Macmillan, 1972.

Brown, Terence: *Northern Voices. Poets From Ulster*. Gill and Macmillan, 1975.

'The Eagle and the Truth. Poetry in Ulster', *Lines Review*, Nos 52/53, May 1975, pp 95-101.

Browne, J.N.: 'Poetry in Ulster' in *The Arts in Ulster*, ed Sam Hanna Bell, Nesca A. Robb and John Hewitt, Harrap, 1951, pp 131-50.

Carney, James: *The Irish Bardic Poet*. Dolmen Press, 1967.

Deane, Seamus: 'The Writer and the Troubles', *Threshold*, No 25, Summer, 1974, pp 13-17.

'Irish Poetry and Irish Nationalism' in *Two Decades of Irish Writing*, ed Douglas Dunn. Carcanet Press, 1975, pp 4-22.

Donoghue, Denis: 'Now and in Ireland: The Literature of Troubles', *Hibernia*, 11th May 1978, pp 16-17.

Dunn, Douglas: ed *Two Decades of Irish Writing*. Carcanet Press, 1975.

'The Speckled Hill, the Plover's Shore: Northern Irish Poetry Today', *Encounter*, Vol XLI, No 6, Dec 1963, pp

Fiacc, Padraic: ed *The Wearing of the Black*. An anthology of contemporary Ulster poetry. Blackstaff Press, 1974.

Foster, John Wilson: *Forces and Themes in Ulster Fiction*. Gill and Macmillan, 1974.

Fullwood, Daphne and Edwards, Oliver: 'Ulster Poetry Since 1900', *Rann*, No 20, June 1953, pp 19-34.

Greacen, Robert: ed. *Poems from Ulster*. Anthology. Belfast, 1941.

ed *Northern Harvest*. Anthology of Ulster Writing. Belfast, 1944.

Even Without Irene. Autobiography. Dolmen Press, 1969.

Group, The: 'The Belfast Group: A Symposium', *The Honest Ulsterman*, No 53, Nov/Dec 1976, pp 53-63.

Hewitt, John: *Rhyming Weavers*, and other country poets of Antrim and Down. Blackstaff Press, 1974.

'Poetry of Ulster: A Survey', *Poetry Ireland*, No 8, Jan 1950, pp 3-10.

'The Course of Writing in Ulster', *Rann*, No 20, June 1953, pp 43-52.

Liddy, James: 'Ulster Poets and the Catholic Muse', *Eire/Ireland*, Winter 1978, pp 126-37. (On Fiacc, Montague and Heaney.)

Longley, Michael: 'Poetry', in *Causeway. The Arts in Ulster*, ed Michael Longley. Arts Council, 1971, pp 95-109.

Mahon, Derek: 'Poetry in Northern Ireland', *Twentieth Century Studies*, No 4, Nov 1970, pp 89-93.

Redshaw, Thomas Dillon: 'Ri, as in Regional: Three Ulster Poets', *Eire/Ireland*, Summer 1974, pp 41-64. (On Heaney, Deane and Montague).

Sergeant, Howard: 'Ulster Regionalism', *Rann*, No 20, June 1953, pp 3-7.

Simmons, James: ed: *Ten Irish Poets*. An anthology. Carcanet Press, 1974.

Acknowledgements

Grateful acknowledgement is made to:

Carcanet Press Ltd for permission to reprint the following poems by George Buchanan: 'Lyle Donaghy, poet, 1902-1969', 'Revolutionary Revolution', 'Knowledge-workers' and 'The Cabinet' from *Minute-Book of a City* (1972); 'I Suddenly...', 'Song for Straphangers', 'A Speaker in the Square', 'A Churchman Speaks', 'Lewis Mumford' and 'Advancing Years' from *Inside Traffic* (1976); Chatto & Windus Ltd and the author for permission to reprint the following poems by Roy McFadden; 'Bigamy' and 'Contemplations of Mary' from *The Garryowen* (1971); Dolmen Press Ltd for permission to reprint the following poems by John Montague: 'A Drink of Milk' and 'A Welcoming Party' from *Poisoned Lands* (1977); 'Summer Storm' and 'The Same Gesture' from *Tides* (1970); 'Like Dolmens Round My Childhood the Old People', 'A Lost Tradition', 'The Siege of Mullingar' and 'The Cage' from *The Rough Field* (1972); 'Dowager' and 'Small Secrets' from *A Slow Dance* (1975); 'Herbert St Revisited' and 'The Point' from *The Great Cloak* (1978); for permission to reprint the following poems by Seamus Deane: 'A Schooling', 'Fording the River' and 'The Brethren' from *Rumours* (1977); Faber & Faber Ltd for permission to reprint the following poems by Louis MacNeice: 'Prayer Before Birth', 'Carrickfergus', 'Autobiography', 'When We Were Children', 'Sunday Morning', 'Snow', 'Death of an Old Lady', 'Death of an Actress', 'Bagpipe Music', 'Conversation', 'Coda', 'The Sunlight on the Garden', 'Meeting Point', 'The Introduction', 'Night-Club', 'Entirely', 'The Truisms', 'The Taxis', 'Charon' and 'Thalassa' from *Collected Poems* (1969); for permission to reprint the following poems by Seamus Heaney: 'Follower' from *Death of a Naturalist* (1966); 'The Peninsula',

'Bogland', 'Undine' and 'The Wife's Tale' from *Door Into the Dark* (1969); 'The Tollund Man' and 'Wedding Day' from *Wintering Out* (1972); 'Mossbawn: Two Poems in Dedication', 'Strange Fruit', 'from Whatever You Say, Say Nothing' and 'Exposure' from *North* (1975);

for permission to reprint the following poems by Tom Paulin: 'Settlers', 'Under the Eyes', 'A New Society', 'Monumental Masons' and 'Deceased Effects' from *A State of Justice* (1977);

for permission to reprint the following poems by Paul Muldoon: 'Dancers at the Moy', 'The Field Hospital' and 'Wind and Tree' from *New Weather* (1973); 'The Centaurs', 'The Merman', 'Duffy's Circus', 'The Mixed Marriage' and 'Ma' from *Mules* (1977);

Gaberbocchus Press Ltd and the author for permission to reprint the following poems by George Buchanan; 'War-and-Peace' from *Bodily Responses* (1958); 'Conversation With Strangers' from *Conversation With Strangers* (1961);

Goldsmith Press and the author for permission to reprint the following poems by Padraic Fiacc: 'Gloss' and 'First Movement' from *Odour of Blood* (1973);

Victor Gollancz Ltd for permission to reprint the following poems by Michael Longley: 'Swans Mating', 'Caravan', 'The Adulterer' and 'Wounds' from *An Exploded View* (1973); 'The Goose', 'Company' and 'Fleance' from *Man Lying on a Wall* (1976);

Holysmoke Press and the author for permission to reprint the following poems by Tom Matthews: 'Private But Sulphurous', 'Happy Arabia', 'Robert Sat', 'Cowboy Film' and 'Even the Whales' from *Dr. Wilson as an Arab* (1974);

Irish Academic Press and the author for permission to reprint the following poems by Seamus Deane: 'Return' and 'Roots' from *Gradual Wars* (1972);

Macmillan Ltd and the author for permission to reprint the following poems by Michael Longley: 'Graffiti', 'Circe', 'Epithalamion', 'No Continuing City' and 'In Memoriam' from *No Continuing City* (1969);

Oxford University Press Ltd for permission to reprint the following poems by W. R. Rodgers: 'Words', 'The Lovers', 'The Party' and 'Field Day' from *Collected Poems* (1971); for permission to reprint the following poems by Derek Mahon: 'In Carrowdore Churchyard', 'Death of a Film Star' (here re-titled 'The Death of Marilyn Monroe'), 'An Unborn Child', 'In Belfast', 'Day Trip to Donegal' and 'As God is my Judge' from *Night-Crossing* (1968); 'Ecclesiastes', 'As It Should Be', 'After Cavafy' (here re-

titled 'Poem Beginning With a Line by Cavafy'), and 'Gipsies
Revisited' from *Lives* (1972); 'The Snow Party' and 'A Disused
Shed in Co. Wexford' from *The Snow Party* (1975);

for permission to reprint the following poems by Frank Ormsby: 'My
Friend Havelock Ellis', 'Winter Offerings', 'Moving In', 'A Day in
August' and 'Passing the Crematorium' from *A Store of Candles*
(1977);

Routledge Ltd and the author for permission to reprint the following
poems by Roy McFadden: 'Epithalamium' and 'Letter to an Irish
Novelist' (here re-titled 'First Letter to an Irish Novelist') from
Flowers for a Lady (1945);

Secker & Warburg for permission to reprint the following poems by
W. R. Rodgers: 'Stormy Night', 'The Net', 'Lent', 'The Swan' and
excerpts from 'Resurrection' from *Europa and the Bull* (1952);

for permission to reprint the following poems by William Peskett:
'The Question of Time', 'Star and Sea', 'The Inheritors', 'Bottles
in the Zoological Museum' and 'Window Dressing' from *The
Night-owl's Dissection* (1975);

NOTE ON REVISIONS

A number of authors' revisions and amendments have been in-
corporated in this anthology. Roy McFadden has rewritten parts of
'Epithalamium' and 'Letter to an Irish Novelist' and has retitled the
latter as 'First Letter to an Irish Novelist'; he has also amended two
lines in 'Bigamy', a section of the sequence 'Memories of China-
town'. Derek Mahon has re-titled 'Death of an Actress' as 'The
Death of Marilyn Monroe', and 'After Cavafy' as 'Poem Beginning
with a Line by Cavafy', omitted the third stanza of the original
version of 'Day Trip to Donegal' and altered words or lines in 'In
Carrowdore Churchyard', 'Gipsies Revisited' and 'A Disused Shed in
Co. Wexford'.

Index